# FACT:

"Inside every business, (large or small) is an opportunity to uncover thousands, even hundreds of thousands of dollars in hidden and/or neglected profits & value!"

~Brian Kaskavalciyan

***What People Are Saying:***

"In his book DOUBLE YOUR PROFITS, Brian has done a praiseworthy job of taking high value marketing concepts and strategies - including some of my own origination - to the tactical level, for practical and instant, paint by numbers implementation. It's a book to be used, not merely read, by a guy who is in the trenches with clients in service businesses, bringing in customers and multiplying customers by referrals."

**Dan. S. Kennedy**
Author, No. B.S. Price Strategy, No B.S. Trust-Based Marketing;
Consultant, Direct-Response Copywriter. www.NoBSBooks.com

"Much of increasing profits comes from simple ideas that are often overlooked or underestimated. Listen closely to what Brian shares in this book - it will change your bottom line!"

**Ali Brown**
Entrepreneur Mentor, Featured on ABC's "Secret Millionaire"

"Brian has crafted an ideal sales and marketing guide with strategies that you can put into action right away."

**Andrea Waltz**
Co-author of "Go For No!"

"There is absolutely no reason you shouldn't be making more sales and earning more profits during these uncertain economic times! And this book provides a step-by-step roadmap to do just that."

**RJon Robins**
www.HowToManageASmallLawFirm.com

"In today's highly competitive marketplace, every customer is important and every dollar is critical. In this must-read book, Brian lays out an easy-to-follow, easy-to-implement, step-by-step system that enables any business to uncover untapped sales and profits that flow directly to the bottom line."

**Martin Howey**
CEO, TopLine Business Solutions

"This book was written to be used. Clear examples, excellent advice, this is a must-read for any business owner. I can't recommend this book enough."

**Andrew Cass**
Certified Dan Kennedy Business Advisor, Miami FL

"I can't think of even one business owner who won't benefit from the strategies laid out in this book. That's why I'm going to recommend it to everyone I know."

**Melanie Benson Strick**
America's Leading Authority on Optimum Performance

"Brian's advice is invaluable! He creates excitement and provides a fresh perspective with his systematic approach. Brian has provided me and my medical practice with practical ideas that have helped me retain patients and grow my practice."

**Dr. Kenneth Cheng**
Co-Founder, Newport Medical Consultants

"As a direct response copywriter and author myself, there aren't very many people whose advice I value or trust. Brian is one of the few people who understand how to grow a business' profits using results-driven marketing strategies and how to write copy that sells!"

**Bill Quinn**
Internet Marketing Expert, Copywriter & Author

"This book is an excellent resource for all business owners. After 12 years of owning my business, I think I "know it all." Brian's book has new twists on important, fundamental business practices that you can't ignore! A helpful tool for me to keep growing my business!

**Eric Perry, President**
The Printmedia Companies of Southern California

"I never really stopped to think about LVC (Lifetime Value of a Client); this book really opened my eyes to the importance of maintaining a constant communication flow with those people who have already purchased my services. They will be in the forefront of my marketing efforts going forward."

**Robert J. Casillas,** CPA

"As I went through these pages I saw many things I'm already doing. But I was amazed to discover how many things I'm not doing - but will do now! The resources found throughout the book are easily worth 100 times the price of the book. I now use his system regularly and I do recommend this book for any business owner"

**Jim Moazez**
VR Business Brokers

"This book is simply powerful and to the point. It does not matter if you are an experienced businessman or just opening your door, you must have Brian's input to succeed."

**Dr. Gilbert Youdeem, D.C., QME, CCSP**
TheChiropracticVillage.com

"As always, your advice has opened my eyes to identifying new avenues within my business that will allow me to greatly increase my revenue without increasing my expenses. The advice you provide is like having a business coach reviewing my sales and marketing plan on an ongoing basis. Each time I review your book, it challenges me to take the steps necessary to make my business competitive and - most importantly - to increase my sales. Thanks for providing your insight; it is exactly what a growing business needs."

**Larry Mandell**
President, Pacific Genesis

"How to Double Your Business' Profits in Six Months or Less is a "must read" for any business owner or manager. Brian's recommended marketing strategies are simple to understand and easy to implement without any overt risk. The marketing tools explained in this book are based on solid, fundamental principles which are often ignored in the day-to-day operations of a business."

**Joseph A. Maleki, Esq.**
Maleki & Associates

"The comparison of a client base to a herd and the whole "Cash Cow Ranch" scenario is brilliant! I can't think of a better or clearer way to explain the importance of your existing clients."

**Dave Bocks**
Dave Bocks & Associates Marketing

## ACKNOWLEDGEMENTS AND GRATITUDE

The strategies and ideas contained in this book are not only my own. These are the same strategies that make up the basic strategic marketing principles that come from the absolute masters of marketing...people like Claude Hopkins, David Ogilvy, John Caples, Jay Abraham and my personal mentor, Dan S. Kennedy.

For years I have been - and continue to be - a serious student of the marketing masters. Of the marketing masters I credit above, it wouldn't be right if I didn't use this opportunity to give Mr. Kennedy special acknowledgment for all he has done for me, and the countless other entrepreneurs he influences every year.

Mr. Kennedy is one of the greatest entrepreneurial minds living today. I've told him he is the greatest teacher of self-reliance of our generation. He has authored 13 books. He is the highest paid copywriter in the country - with minimum fees between $75,000 and $120,000 (plus royalties) for a single sales letter... if you can hire him! As a speaker, he has shared the stage with former presidents, professional athletes and other leaders in the areas of personal and professional development. For many years, I have been fortunate to be a private client and be personally coached and mentored by Mr. Kennedy.

Mr. Kennedy's teachings, advice and philosophies have had such a profound (and profitable) effect on me that I can honestly say I wouldn't be where I am today without him, and I am grateful for all he has done - and continues to do - for entrepreneurs and marketers of all types.

# HOW TO DOUBLE YOUR PROFITS IN 6 MONTHS OR LESS

**8 Powerful Profit-Multiplying Strategies That Any Business - Regardless of Size - Can Immediately Implement and Profit From**

BRIAN KASKAVALCIYAN

**This book is available at quantity discounts for bulk purchases. Please go to www.DoubleYourProfitBook.com for more information or call 888-215-4268.**

ISBN: 978-0-9858402-0-4 (Paperback)
ISBN: 978-0-9858402-1-1 (eBook)

Printed in the United States of America
Cover design by: Ana Lopez | www.anaurbana.com

DISCLAIMER AND/OR LEGAL NOTICES

This publication is designed to provide accurate and authoritative information in regard to the subject matter covered. It is sold with the understanding that the publisher is not engaged in rendering legal, accounting or other professional services. If legal advice or other expert assistance is required, the services of a competent professional should be sought. While the publisher and the author have used their best efforts in preparing this book, they make no representations or warranties with respect to the accuracy or completeness of the contents of this book. The advice and strategies contained herein may not be suitable for your situation. You should consult a professional where appropriate. Neither the publisher or the author shall be liable for any loss of profit or any other commercial damages, including but not limited to special, incidental, consequential, or other damages. The purchaser or reader of this publication assumes responsibility for the use of these materials and information. Adherence to all applicable laws and regulations, both advertising and all other aspects of doing business in the United States or any other jurisdiction, is the sole responsibility of the purchaser or reader.

# YOUR $19,000 NO-RISK MONEY BACK GUARANTEE

Don't let the fact that you purchased this book at its ridiculously low cover price discount its value to you. This little book is easily worth thousands of times its cover price to you.

However, the biggest investment you're going to make with this book is not the paltry cover price. It's the time to read it, absorb its content and implement the strategies contained within.

I take your time very seriously. I don't want this to be just another book you wasted your time and money on that gets glanced over and tossed aside. So to prove my commitment to you, this book comes with '**NO RISK**' **Money Back Guarantee**. Here it is: If you read this book and the strategies and tactics it contains don't produce at least $19,000 in extra profits for your business, you can return it for a full refund! That's right, if this book does not produce a 1,000% return on your investment let us know ASAP; you can return it with proof of purchase and we'll immediately refund your money... no matter where or when you purchased it... no questions asked!

**Brian Kaskavalciyan**

## *TO JOHN & ROSE*

*It takes a lot of patience and unconditional love to raise a pain in the a** like me - and these two did it (continue to do it) without complaint.*

# CONTENTS

**SECTION THREE: How To Effectively And Profitably Acquire New Clients**



**SECTION FOUR: Putting It Together For Maximum Profit!**

# PREFACE

Dear Reader,

I'm not sure how you found your way to this book, but I'm happy that you're here. I truly believe that it can change your business, and your life; otherwise I wouldn't have wasted my time creating it.

You've probably never heard of me, but I think after reading this book, you'll be glad you did.

Since publishing the first edition of this book much has happened in the economy. We've gone from a thriving business environment with less than 5% unemployment and money flowing in the streets to the worst economic conditions since the Great Depression. Yes, some businesses have been turned upside down, shut down and closed their doors forever; fortunes have been reversed. BUT at the same time there are countless businesses that are THRIVING in this environment.

I am fortunate to work with many clients whose businesses have grown DESPITE the challenging economic times. For example, I have a client who started his business in April of 2009 with $7,000 and as of this writing is on track to do $5+ million dollars in 2011. He has over 40 employees, the business is debt free. The best part is that he's now semi-retired, working "in" his business only on Wednesday afternoons, and all of this was accomplished in less than 30 months!

I have another client whose business has exploded in the last year. Going from barely six figures in revenues in 2009 to over $600,000 last year 2011, and on track to do over $1,000,000 in 2012. Want more proof or encouragement? Just look at this year's *Inc. 500* list.

We can go back and forth for days on the reasons why some businesses make it and some don't. Admittedly, some businesses are just destined to fail. In fact, after reading this book you'll start to recognize some of the signs. But, I feel the bigger issue here is our mindset about the whole thing.

Lately, when speaking with groups, I will start off by acknowledging that we can't avoid the "elephant in the room" (the economy). However, I firmly believe that my success or failure is up to ME, and your success or failure is up to YOU. This is a much broader conversation than we can have here. But I'll say to you what I say to anyone about this subject: "*We can't avoid the current economic conditions, but we can look at it as opportunity or defeat.*" And I can tell you with certainty that whichever YOU choose will be *right for YOU.*

By picking up this book you might be looking for answers, new information, ideas, strategies, tactics, tools and advice for growing your business and your profits. This is good, this is healthy, and this is having the attitude that regardless of what's happening "out there" you are going to take care of what's happening in and around you.

You may have picked up this book hoping that it will provide a quick fix for your business's problems. I'm sorry to say that I know of no such thing - including this book - trust me, I've been looking for nearly 20 years.

However, I will tell you this - in fact I'll guarantee it - if you are willing to do the "work" that is required of you and follow the advice provided within these pages, you will find this book to be an invaluable tool for your success. If you are willing to do the work I lay out on these pages you will make more money – regardless of the economy.

Incidentally, what I just said is usually a big "no-no", especially on the first page. I told you right up front that you are going to have to do some work. Most authors of books like this don't want to tell you that, because quite frankly a lot less people will buy it. The truth is that if you want to double your profits, build a successful company, and live the life of your dreams... it's actually quite simple but, it's not going to be "easy," it will require real work... but you can definitely do it.

With that said, there are a few things about me you should know before we go any further.

As of this writing, I have started, grown and managed seven businesses. I have bought businesses and sold businesses. I've had no employees and had over 100. I've generated tens of millions of dollars in sales. Acquired thousands of customers and clients. I've even developed a company from scratch into a multi-million dollar national franchise company. I can proudly say that I have relied on myself and the businesses I've created to feed me and my family (quite nicely) uninterrupted since 1993.

But, it hasn't been all sunshine and rainbows. I've had more sleepless nights than I can count. I've made some very painful and expensive mistakes along the way. I've even lost everything and had to rebuild from scratch.

Today I'm involved in a number of businesses, but my main role is as the founder and lead marketing strategist for ***g|Four Marketing Group Inc.*** My company provides a host of products and services (primarily designed around profiting from creating "Customers for Life") to businesses of all kinds that are interested in substantially increasing their sales, increasing profits, increasing the owner(s)' free time, increasing market value, and/or readying a business for sale.

Like you, I'm in the trenches every day generating leads, acquiring new customers, managing employees, working to meet payroll, satisfy customers and solving real business problems.

**You should know that even though I've been at this a long time, I'm still a devoted student of money-making and success strategies**. Over the years (as a student), I've invested well over $100,000 and *thousands of hours* in my "education". I *still* devour dozens of books, articles, magazines and newsletters every year on marketing, entrepreneurship, sales, success and wealth creation and attend high-level marketing training programs on a regular basis.

**More importantly - unlike a lot of consultants, speakers and authors** - my experiences are in "real" businesses. I don't consult or dispense advice merely because of the books I've read or some silly weekend "be a consultant" training program or "coaching certification." My advice, strategies and tactics have all been battle-tested in my own businesses - and my clients' businesses - and have been used to add PROFITS, CUSTOMERS and VALUE.

I want you to know all this because I think it makes this book more valuable to you. I didn't write this book to become a New York Times bestselling author; sure, it would be nice but, it's not my intention. I didn't write it for the measly buck or two I'll make in royalties. My motivation is to help you achieve what you want. I learned a long time ago that if I help enough people get what they want, then I'll get what I want. So the more value I can add to your life... the more value I'll add to mine.

Not knowing how you came across this book, I can only assume that you're not satisfied with the amount of profit you're currently earning and you want to double - or substantially increase - the profits and value of your business.

If this is true, then you've come to the right place, because this book has one singular purpose – **to double the profits of your business over the next 180 days!**

Regardless if your business is currently losing money or making money... your profits are $20,000 or $2,000,000 a year... your business is new or established... your business is B2B (business to business) or B2C (business to consumer), a service business, a professional practice, a retail store or a restaurant... if you are a commissioned salesperson, manufacturer's rep or contractor... <u>these strategies will work for you and for your business.</u>

I'm going to take a rather unorthodox approach to get you there. But, I assure you that if you follow me step-by-step through each of the exercises in this book, you can have no other logical outcome than to double (or substantially increase) your profits.

**Before we get started, I should warn you:** my views and my approach to marketing your business and multiplying your profits are probably quite different than what you, your staff, your colleagues, your family or your friends might think *successful* marketing is.

**I am blunt and straightforward, and I am driven by results.** I don't tell my clients what they want to hear; rather, I tell them what they need to hear in order to get the outcome they desire. <u>I am not</u>

going to treat you any differently.

This offends some, but quite frankly, I'm not paid to be a friend, I am paid to produce results.

I ask that you read this book with an open mind. I won't ask you to blindly believe what's on these pages, but I would ask you to look at each section and ask yourself the questions: *"What if this is true?"* and, *"How can I apply this to my business?"*

I promise that if you will honestly take the time to go through this book from start to finish (without skimming or skipping), think about what you read from a logical place (rather than emotional), complete the exercises and fill-in-the-blank worksheets and implement these strategies and tactics, you will be more effective, efficient and successful in whatever business you are in.

I am excited for you. I am confident that the ideas and strategies presented here will undoubtedly open your eyes to new possibilities and help you rise to new levels of business and personal success.

Dedicated to your success,

**Brian Kaskavalciyan**
**February, 2012**
**Miami, Florida**

# HOW TO USE THIS BOOK

As a highly-paid marketing strategist and consultant, people come to me generally because [a] they have a problem they need to solve (not making enough money, they work to hard or too much, they want to sell their business but don't know how) or [b] they have an opportunity they want to take advantage of such as a new business opportunity or expanding their current business.

Ironically, many of these people are searching for some complex, high-tech, almost magical, solution to their problem. And often the answer to their question (and yours) is really much simpler than they - or you - ever imagined.

Inside this book you'll find a few of our most powerful profit-improvement strategies that you can apply to your business today.

What I have attempted to do on the following pages is to take the same ***basic*** path that I would use as your strategist/consultant (which, by the way, would require a minimum investment of $6,750.00 a day) to uncover hidden or neglected opportunities in yours/my clients' businesses and spell them out for you in a simple, straightforward and - most importantly – easy-to-implement fashion.

You will find the strategies in their most basic form with a few simple tactics, so they will be easy to understand and implement. I have included exercises, action steps - and most importantly - resources that will allow you to execute these strategies in your business.

I have left out many other more-advanced strategies that I feel are beyond the scope and intent of this book.

I've also not offering strategies on increasing profits by cost cutting, implementing efficiencies, etc - this book is about GROWTH.

Most of the strategies/tactics will not require you to spend any more money than you do now. In fact, most of the strategies will not require you to spend more than just a few hours of your time to implement in your business.

It's important that you understand that the information included in this book is a compilation of time-tested, proven marketing (and business development) strategies and tactics. I have actually used every one of these strategies in my own businesses - and in my clients' businesses - to immediately add PROFITS, CUSTOMERS and VALUE.

## GETTING THE MOST OUT OF THIS BOOK

If you really want to get the most out of this book, it will require commitment and focused action; it must be an interactive - not passive - event. What I mean by this is that you should treat this book like a workbook. (Remember this book is not about theories or ideas. This book is about strategies and tactics - that if implemented - WILL significantly increase your profits.) Don't be afraid to write in it, fill out the worksheets, take notes, jot down ideas, use a highlighter... whatever.

I want you to beat it up! In fact, if you do beat up the book and would like a clean copy for your library – no problem; contact my office and I'll be happy to send you a clean one **at no charge**. The only thing I'll ask in return is a picture of the book (marked up) and the details of how this book helped your business or your life. (I'll post your story on this book's website to encourage other readers!)

With your purchase of this book, you'll get access to its companion site - **www.DoubleYourProfitBook.com -** which I've loaded with over $576.00 in additional tools and resources to help you increase your business's profits. If you're close to a computer go to: www.DoubleYourProfitBook.com and register your book now.

## HOW THIS BOOK IS DESIGNED

This book is divided into four sections:

## SECTION 1:

### Setting the Stage for Dramatically Increasing Your Profits

This first section addresses the number one obstacle to dramatically increased profits that I find when working with business owners.

*Their attitudes, beliefs and mindsets...what I'll call the "head trip" stuff.*

For the most part, no matter how big or small a business, we as owners all have preconceived ideas about what is possible with our customers, with our market, with our industry, with our business and what is not.

We all believe we have a complete understanding of why our customers act or react in a certain way... how our business, our customer, our market, our product or service... is somehow uniquely different from everyone else's.

In most cases, we are wrong. So these attitudes and self-limiting beliefs don't allow us to get what we want from our business or from our life.

I've realized that if I don't address these issues with the client/ business owner(s) <u>first</u>, it won't matter what million-dollar suggestions are made, what profit-producing plans are designed, what winning marketing materials are created... none of it will be effective or implemented without the right mindsets.

Don't make any early judgments about this section; I guarantee you will enjoy it!

## SECTION 2:

### Uncovering the Hidden Riches Lying Dormant and Neglected Within Your Business

In almost every business - small, medium or large - there are hidden, neglected riches just waiting to be uncovered and liberated. This is generally the area where I can uncover the most value and profit from a business.

In this section I'll introduce you to 4 simple strategies that you can use to generate immediate and sustainable profits from your existing customers.

It's incredible to me how many business owners just let tens of thousands or even hundreds of thousands of dollars per year in profits go down the drain! When you're done with this section you'll understand where the real profit value and potential is in your business.

## SECTION 3:

### How to Effectively and Profitably Acquire New Clients!

Most small business owners waste tons of money on ineffective tactics trying to get new customers. In this section we will focus on 4 strategies that will super-charge your lead-generation efforts.

## SECTION 4:

### Putting It All Together for Maximum Profit!

The final section will summarize all that you have learned and help you put together a plan of ACTION! Again, this book is not designed to be a passive experience. If you are really serious about substantially increasing your profits, you must put together a plan of attack and then take massive action. This section will give you the tools you'll need to be able to implement all that you have learned from this book.

## EXAMPLES, RESOURCES AND ACTION STEPS

One of the most powerful elements of this book will be examples of how each strategy could be executed by 4 major business categories. (The businesses shown in parentheses are examples of the types of businesses that would fall under each category; it is by no means a complete list.) They are: 1) **Retail** (Menswear/Ladies, Jewelry, Beauty Supply, Florist); 2) **Service** (Auto Repair, Contractor, Carpet Cleaning, Maid Service, Computer Repair, Hair Salon, Plumbing); 3) **Restaurant** (Fast Food, Fine Dining, Ice Cream shop); 4)

**Professional Services** (CPA, Doctor, Lawyer, Consultant).

Finally, throughout this book you will find resources, action steps and big ideas. These are meant to take you out of the pages of this book and actually assist you in implementing the ideas for maximum profits. You'll also find a number of QR Codes that look like this:

From your smartphone (iPhone) you scan the code and it will take you to the resource mentioned. You can download a QR code reader at the iTunes App Store.

Many of these tools and resources will be found at this books website. In order to unlock all of the resources please register your book.

## REGISTER YOUR BOOK NOW AT:

www.DoubleYourProfitBook.com/register

Or scan this code with your Smartphone.

# INTRODUCTION

## Are You Working Too Hard, For Too Little?

I have been asked why I've made the focus of this book profit. It's simple really... the majority of entrepreneurs I meet are working way too hard for far too little and they deserve a pay raise!

Like many business owners, you may have started out with the idea that if you had your own business, it would afford you some new level of control over your life. But as your business grew, you got pulled in many different directions. And pretty soon, you found yourself working for IT, rather than *it* working for YOU.

People don't realize that a business has a dangerous tendency of taking on a life of its own. If you're not careful, the entity that you gave life to and kept alive with your blood, sweat and tears, will turn on you and trap you. It will make you its *servant*, while *it* becomes the *master*.

If you've seen the movie *The Matrix,* this is what the machines did to the humans. The humans created the machines, but over time the machines eventually took over. They became the masters of the earth, while humans became batteries to keep them alive.

Unfortunately when this happens, it's hard to get out from under it. Uncertainty, lack of focus and lack of confidence on the business owner's part, almost certainly leads to fear. Fear makes us look at people, situations - even opportunities - emotionally, rather than logically, and that is not a good place from which to make decisions or run a business.

**Fortunately it doesn't have to be this way.** The good news is that almost without exception, inside of every business are hidden riches... gold, platinum and diamond mines of opportunity that are just waiting to be intelligently and strategically cultivated to reap the rewards.

In this book we are going to focus on just one aspect of the hidden riches (the riches we find are not always financial) in your business and that is PROFIT - CASH MONEY!

**Why profit?**

- **Profit is the fuel that drives your business. Without profits, your business won't grow.**
- **Without steadily increasing profits, you'll continue working just as hard tomorrow as you are today, with nothing to show for it.**
- **Without profit, you can't hope to pay your employees the wages they deserve.**
- **Without profit, you can't pay yourself what you deserve.**
- **Profit is what allows you to continue serving your clients and building your future.**
- **Profit gives you OPTIONS to pursue those areas of your life and your business that you most enjoy.**

And quite frankly, generating extra profit is not that hard to do!

## WHAT HOLDS US BACK?

You might be saying, "Okay, Brian... this sounds great, but I'm just so busy all day trying to keep up or get "caught up" (if that is ever possible). I want to take my business to the "next level" (whatever that means) so I can make enough money, or free up enough time to be, do, or have something different than we have now, but I just don't have the money, the people to help me or the time."

So many business owners are caught in this trap... trust me I've been there too! But the truth is that most business owners are too "busy" with unproductive, unprofitable $8, $10, $25 an hour activities, making a living and working "in" their business, that they don't have the time or the energy to work "on" their business.

This behavior causes chaos in the business and the business

owner's life; ultimately they spend their days reacting to what's happening, rather than proactively creating what is going to happen.

In our work with business owners, we address these issues to "break through" the limiting behaviors and free the business owner to become a strategic entrepreneur (what we call a Fourth-Stage Entrepreneur™) to run his or her business as an investor would, from the outside looking in.

## A CHALLENGE AND AN OPPORTUNITY

These ideas are beyond the scope of this book, but I introduce them here because it's important to realize that there is a conversation going on in our heads about the current state of our business and it's not always moving us where we think we want to go.

This presents us with both a challenge and an opportunity. The challenge is that most of this behavior is brought on by beliefs, attitudes and motivations that have been with us for a very long time.

Only you can push them aside and get them out of your way so you can get to work "on" your business. **It's often times harder to solve this problem than it is to execute the strategies that will build your business and massively increase your profits.**

However, this also presents us with an enormous opportunity. The good news for you is that most of your competitors are also so caught up working "in" their businesses, that they don't have any time to focus on growing their business. And the truth is in most cases, they won't be willing to do the "work" it takes to make their business special, to make their business standout and to make their business worthy of a huge increase in profits!

With the information in this book, you'll be on your way to learning the skill of marketing. Don't worry; this is a skill you can master. Once you're done with this book, the basic marketing skills you will have learned and implemented in your business will give you freedom and options, while at the same time it won't be long before you've made your competition irrelevant and you've begun to capitalize on opportunities you never noticed before. You'll soon see how relatively simple it is to become the dominant business of your type in your market.

## MONEY, MONEY, MONEY

*"Until and unless you understand that money is the root of all good, you ask for your own destruction. When money ceases to be the tool by which men deal with one another, then men become the tools of men. Blood, whips, and guns – or dollars. Take your choice-there is no other."*

**Ayn Rand**
**Author, Atlas Shrugged**

Before moving on, I feel we must address the money "issue".

People have asked me why this book is so focused on money. "Doesn't it seem selfish, insignificant or petty to be focused solely on profit?" they ask.

I have two responses to those questions.

First, let me immediately make the point that the main motivating reason to be in whatever business you're in should be **profit**.

If it's not, you don't belong in business for yourself.

Yet as a consultant, I find all sorts of people in all types of businesses who are not primarily profit motivated. They've got their priorities mixed up. Business decisions made with something other than profit as the prime consideration are almost certain to be bad decisions.

Here is why *I* believe your business exists. In fact, I'm going to ask you to accept my definition, at least while you are reading this book:

Here it is in first person:

**"My business exists**
**to satisfy my needs,**
**to fund my lifestyle**
**and to give me the ability**
**to live the life I want to live."**

Now some of you are reading this and thinking this sounds awfully selfish and self-serving - and I would agree - because it is. Your business must be this way, or else!

Here's one of the biggest lessons I learned from my mentor, Dan Kennedy:

**Your business's purpose is:**

- NOT to provide jobs
- NOT to pay taxes
- NOT to support the community
- NOT to improve customers' lives
- NOT to improve employees' lives

It may do all of these things (to one degree or another), but only as a by-product of achieving its true purpose. Read that again, *"only as a by-product of achieving its true purpose"*. And its true purpose is - *satisfying YOUR needs.*

Think about it...

How can you provide jobs if your business can't support you and your family?

How can your business support the community if it can't support you and your family?

How can you improve the lives of your customers or employees if you can't improve your own life, or don't live the life you want to live?

If your business exists because you feel some moral obligation to any of the above (or something else), you are in deep trouble and this book is not going to help you.

I find that often times we forget the real reason our business exists.

## YOU MUST GET PAST YOUR PRECONCEPTIONS ABOUT MONEY

Second, I would challenge you to look past your preconceptions about money. I won't pretend that I am an expert on the complete psychology of money. What I do understand of it is that there are people who make money into something greater than it really is.

Some even go so far as using the Bible to make money a bad thing by believing the Bible says that 'money is the root of all evil.' The scripture actually says:

***"For the love of money is a root of all kinds of evil."***
1 Timothy 6:10

The people who use that scripture as a warning conveniently leave out the most important 4 words: "***For the love of***". If you include those 4 little words, the meaning of the scripture is very different.

I do not promote, nor practice the love of money. **Money/profit is simply recognition for services rendered**. The more people you serve - the more profit you'll earn. The more value you provide the people you serve - the more money you'll make... better, EARN. If the service you are providing is moral and ethical and has your customers' best interests foremost in mind, then profit is your <u>just</u> reward!

Many people fear what is going to happen to them once they have money. I have battled this fear myself, but I remember the old saying that goes: money - like alcohol - makes a good man better, and a bad man worse. So, if you are good-hearted, ethical and honorable today, doubling your profits doesn't mean that all of a sudden your character will somehow magically change. The only difference will be that the money will give you many more <u>***options***</u>.

So, for the sake of argument and for our purposes throughout the rest of this book, let's not make money a "good" thing or a "bad" thing... let's not make it "right" or "wrong"... let's just accept it for what it is – <u>the way we are rewarded for the service we provide the world and as a means for getting the things we need and want</u>.

**With that said... let's get to work!**

# SECTION

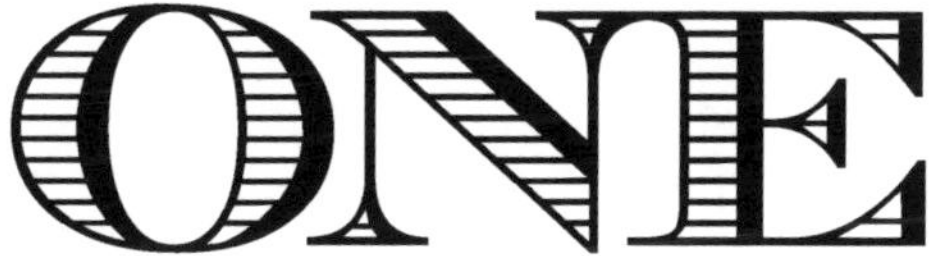

## SETTING THE STAGE FOR DRAMATICALLY INCREASING YOUR PROFITS

*"There is no passion to be found in playing small - in settling for a life that is less than the one you are capable of living."*

Nelson Mandela

# CHAPTER 1

## To Double Your Profits, You've Got To Understand "The Ultimate Success Formula"

This book is designed with one singular purpose in mind... to double the profits of your business in 6 months or less. However, the beauty of this system is that it is completely driven by you! I am only suggesting a possible outcome and timeframe. Some reading this book will be thrilled with a 20% increase, while others may be looking for 300%. Some will want to accomplish this in 3 months and some in 12 months; either way... the same system, strategies and tools will work for you.

Instead of just writing out the strategies and tactics you could use to accomplish this (which would be a much easier book to write than this one), I felt I would be doing you a disservice if I didn't help you with the "head trip" stuff first.

You see, for most business owners the idea of doubling profits - legally and ethically- is often met with resistance. But not the usual outward resistance... no, I'm talking about the hidden, subconscious resistance that comes from our old programming. This resistance comes in many forms, including self-doubt, resignation and uncertainty.

I have realized that when working with my private clients, if I don't address the "head trip" issues with the owner(s) first, it won't matter what million-dollar suggestions are made, what profit-producing plans are designed, what winning marketing materials are created - none of it will be effective or even implemented without the right mindsets. So I am going to make the same assumption with you and work on the "head trip" stuff first, so that we are both well prepared for what is coming.

You see, the funny thing is that the mechanics of what I will present here are fairly straightforward. They are time-tested strategies that have always worked - and will always work - in growing businesses. The important thing for you to realize is that the strategies don't change... they are constant. What does change - what is not constant - is the people who execute them.

Inside of all of us is a system for getting what we really want, whether we acknowledge it or not. What I have attempted to do is give you an idea of how this system is working so you can use it to accomplish the outcome you desire from this book.

So in this first chapter, I'm going to introduce you to **The Ultimate Success Formula**™. This formula will help you gain a better understanding of what you really want and why you want it and then map out a game plan (process or system) that you can use to not only double your profits, but really get anything you want for your business and your life.

Now I realize this sounds a little fantastic, but I did warn you that I would take you on an unorthodox path to achieving your goal of doubling (or substantially increasing) your profits. At the very beginning, I asked that you read this book with an open mind. I would challenge you to do all of the exercises in this chapter before making any judgments about the formula. Remember, my goal here is to help you double your profits!

Fair enough?

Okay... before I introduce the formula, let me tell you why I have abandoned all the usual and customary goal-setting programs and created my own.

## BECAUSE... TRADITIONAL GOAL-SETTING METHODS DON'T WORK!

How many times have you set a goal, only to fail? You wrote it down like you were supposed to, put a deadline to it, thought about it every day, made "to-do" lists, used "The Secret" and still you didn't achieve it.

I know I have many, many times!

All of the so called goal-setting and achievement "gurus" preach a variation of the same basic formula. Here it is... it may look familiar:

→ Set a goal.

→ Put the goal in writing.

→ Set a time deadline for the attainment of the goal.

→ Develop a plan and work the plan.

→ Visualize a successful result.

→ Maintain a positive attitude.

→ Measure your progress and make adjustments as needed.

→ Persist until you reach your goal.

Sounds good...right?

Does it work? Rarely for me... how about for you? My guess would be that it doesn't and it hasn't.

See, all of this sounds great in a book, in a seminar, or on TV -- except for one problem -- *most people don't achieve their goals using this method*!

## THE EXTRA 15 POUNDS THAT WON'T GO AWAY!

Let me give you a personal example that I think many can relate to about why the traditional formula DOES NOT work:

Since earlier this year, I have managed to gain an extra 15 pounds. I don't like the way I look... I don't like the way I feel... but it's there. My clothes don't fit right, and I'm not in as good of shape as I was just 12 months ago. I can accept the weight and live with it, but I'd really rather not.

Like most people, I would love to find the fastest, easiest way to lose the 15 pounds. If there was a magic pill I could take and wake up tomorrow morning at my ideal weight, I'd take it. But as we all know, unfortunately no such pill exists (at least not in a legal or safe form).

If you listen to the goal-setting, self-help "gurus", they'll tell you to write your goals down, create "to-do" lists that include action items, and even more importantly, a deadline. Some of them will ask you to believe that you can have whatever you want just by thinking "the right way", by visualizing the outcome, or by speaking as if it's already happened.

Have you tried that?

I can write the goal down as many times and in many ways as I want.

*"I want to lose 15 pounds."*

*"I am so happy and grateful now that I am at my ideal weight of 160 pounds."*

*"It is February 3rd and I am at my ideal weight of 160 pounds."*

I can break it down into weekly, daily, hourly activities - on paper. I can repeat the above statements 100 times a day, meditate and visualize.

Will I achieve my goal? Not likely. Why?

Because deep down I know that losing the weight is going to require me to make some changes in my behavior and my choices. It's going to require me to do some work... both emotional and physical.

That's not to say that what I've mentioned above doesn't work. It does; it has its place in achievement of your goals, but only as part of a larger program.

In the grand scheme of things, the work and choices aren't that difficult (just like increasing your profits). According to common sense, Men's Health magazine and my personal trainer, I just have to do 4 things for about 90 days in order to lose the weight:

Eat a little less at each meal. (Easy, right? Just cut the portion by a third or a half.)

Eat healthier. (Eat less French fries, cut out the 1000-calorie Greek salads and eat more fruits, vegetables and raw, unprocessed foods.)

Limit myself to 100 calories of everyday sweets. (Reserve the cookies, cakes or other treats for one day a week.)

Spend just 30 minutes, 4 times a week, on a treadmill, Stairmaster, elliptical or cycle. (Actually breaking a sweat.)

Sounds pretty simple...right?

But I haven't really, completely committed to doing any of it. Oh, I've "tried" to "get started" a few times. Sound familiar?

In real life, doesn't this scenario play out something like this?

**Day Zero:** Set the goal of losing 15 pounds.

**Day One:** Go to the gym and eat less. Tell all of our friends we're on a diet and we're going to lose that weight! Do great and feel great and get excited.

**Day Two:** Oversleep...can't make it to the gym in the morning. We'll go after work. We eat a light lunch, but end up too tired to go to gym after work.

**Day Three:** Get to the gym in the morning and get on the bike. Get to work and a friend calls to ask you to go out after work... so, you end up at your favorite spot, devouring your favorite dinner. But it's okay; you'll make It up tomorrow.

**Day Four to Six:** More of the same, gradually falling back into old habits and patterns.

**Day Seven:** Back to the gym, "OK, I've got to get back on track."

I won't bore you with the rest because you know how it ends. Not only do we not get the desired result, but we have to come up with all kinds of justifications to ourselves (and those around us) for why we failed!

"I'm going to start again on Monday; this is just a bad week."

"Diets don't work for me."

"I've just heard about this new diet."

"I've tried everything to lose weight."

"My whole family is overweight, who am I kidding?"

"I just can't afford a gym membership right now."

I could just keep going with the reasons why, and you could probably help me add a few!

The problem with this is not the fact that you did not reach the goal, but what happens to the normal person who sets a goal to lose weight, make money, get married, buy a house, pay off debts, etc., and doesn't achieve that goal.

After years of the disappointment of not achieving our "goals", we stop believing we can get what we want. We start thinking -- and ultimately believing -- in the recesses of our minds that:

[being, doing or having] ______________ is not possible for me.

I don't deserve to [be, do or have] __________.

I'm not good enough for ___________.

Only people that are ______________ [rich, good looking, come from the right family, etc.] can [be, do or have] ____________.

Once we've done this to ourselves, it's tough to return to a place of positive thought where our desires are achievable. Every time you set a new goal, you are reminded of your past "failures." We feel disappointment, resignation and ultimately, fear about our present and future situation.

We end up <u>reacting</u> to what's happening to us rather than <u>consciously</u>, <u>purposefully</u> and <u>proactively</u> <u>creating</u> <u>our</u> <u>results</u>.

## SO HOW'S "MY" FORMULA DIFFERENT?

So why do you think we don't get what we want? Why haven't I lost the weight? Why aren't you taking the actions necessary for you to get what you want?

From my experience, we end up setting a goal for what we "think" we want. The problem is that we don't understand why we "really" want it. We think we want to lose the weight, but what we really want is to look good in a bathing suit on the beach, so we can look good for our significant other or we don't want to be embarrassed by how we'll look in a bathing suit on the beach.

If you ask enough questions about why someone wants something (goal), the answer will ultimately lead us to *<u>being</u>*, *<u>doing</u>* or *<u>having</u>*

something different than we have now. So, it only makes sense that if you really want to achieve your goal, you have to understand the "be, do and have" of why you want the goal.

This leads to the second reason: If we don't completely understand why we want something, we won't be sufficiently motivated to achieve it - we won't want it bad enough to do everything necessary to bring it about. We won't want it bad enough to get through the obstacles and letdowns we are undoubtedly going to experience on our way to reaching the goal.

You see, when we set a goal, we are almost immediately met with challenges and obstacles. We suffer breakdowns and our determination to succeed is tested. If our underlying motivation is not strong enough, if our reasons why we want the goal aren't clear, then the breakdowns will cause us to give up.

**Here is the truth about getting what we want**: only until something shakes us up with such emotional intensity, with such conviction and with such passion that we have to make it happen... do we get determined enough and serious enough to then "magically" summon the energy, the focus and the willpower to take the actions that must be taken to get what we really want.

Let me say that again, this time with emphasis:

We will not get what we want until something shakes us up with such emotional intensity, with such conviction and with such passion that we **have to** make it happen...

Let's go back to the diet example for a minute. Don't you have a friend who is normally a little overweight and is always on a diet, but when they know they are going on a vacation in X weeks and are going to be on a beach in a bathing suit, they somehow magically trim down? Of course you do - we all do - many times it's us!

Now, admittedly I'm going a little further than I wanted to on this subject, but I really want to make this point. I believe that the strategies and tactics in this book are completely ineffective for you if I don't help you get your head straight first. And because I am committed to helping you double -- or significantly increase -- your profits, I MUST start here.

## THE ULTIMATE SUCCESS FORMULA

Over the next few pages, I'm going to introduce you to a powerful formula for getting anything you want from life. This formula is not entirely my own. It is a combination of observation, study and experience. I am not asking you to blindly believe anything on the following pages; just remember to go through the formula with an open mind.

Before we talk about the formula, let me make a few things clear that I absolutely believe about YOU (even though I don't know you and we will likely never meet).

- ✓ You have everything you need right now to get everything you want.
- ✓ There is nothing inherently "wrong" with you that would prevent you from getting anything you truly want.
- ✓ Deep down inside, you know what you really, truly want.
- ✓ You absolutely deserve to be, do or have whatever you desire.

## VOCABULARY CHANGE

First, I'd like to pull a vocabulary change on you.

The definition of a goal according to the Encarta dictionary is:

**Goal – aim:** something that somebody wants to achieve

I don't like that definition because of the word wants. It suggests that a goal is merely a want. I prefer a word that is more definite.

I prefer the word **OUTCOME**, here is the definition:

**Outcome – result:** the way that something turns out in the end

Do you notice the difference in definitions? One is about something somebody *wants* to achieve the other is about a *result*, the way something is in the end.

For our purposes here and throughout the rest of the book, we aren't going to talk about goals; we are going to talk about outcomes!

WARNING: You may find The Ultimate Success Formula "difficult." You may find it requires more "work" than you may be willing to put in. The truth of it is if you are not mentally prepared, then the rest of this book will be useless to you. There is a reason why the self-help gurus keep their "systems" easy; the reason is that it's much easier to sell to the masses. It's much easier to sell more books when the "work" is perceived to be "easy." But as I said earlier, the "easy" system rarely works. You can fool yourself and pretend to be setting and achieving your desired outcomes... you can go through the motions and make it look good... but in the end you won't get what you truly want.

As an author, I could have taken that route as well; believe me, it would have been so much easier than what I'm doing here. However, I know that it would be a sham. Sure, the contents of this book -- if implemented as presented -- *could* double your profits. But, I would know deep down that if I was to give you the "easy" program, this book wouldn't work for you. Sure it would look good on the outside, but in the end the outcome that I have committed to would not come about for you and I just don't operate that way.

What this system requires you to do is really think and dig deep inside yourself to understand why you really want to increase your profits. To me that is the real "work." So here it is... be bold, believe and have fun.

## STEP 1: UNDERSTANDING AND IDENTIFYING YOUR OUTCOME

*"The best way to predict the future is to create it."*
- **Peter Drucker**

The first step is to clearly define the outcome(s) that you intend - not just want - but what you intend to be, do or have. This is writing down what you desire as an outcome that you have already achieved - not just something you want, not something that would be nice to have, not just a wish, but a clear, concise, measurable outcome that has already been accomplished.

For example:

- "I doubled my profits to $200,000."
- "I increased my client's average transaction to $550."
- "I increased my free time by 2 weeks per year."

- "I purchased a piece of income property."
- "I am happy and healthy at 160 pounds."
- "I am driving my new Aston Martin db9."

When you list the outcomes in the past tense as accomplishments, you trick your mind into believing you're already there. Instead of anticipating all the effort required and all the obstacles between you and the outcome, visualize yourself already being where you want to be. It gives you the mindset you need for success.

Start with just one or two outcomes and stay focused on them for at least 30 days. If after 30 days you feel you're doing well and getting closer to the outcome, then start with another one.

Don't write down a lot of outcomes at the same time. You won't achieve any. The key to getting what you want is staying focused. And it is impossible to focus on fourteen outcomes at the same time.

We can create our lives and we can design the life we want to live. The problem is that we rarely give it enough thought. We get caught up in our day-to-day lives and end up reacting to what's happening to us, rather than proactively creating what will happen to us.

By being able to clearly define the outcome we want, we are able to create a plan - followed by actions - to bring that outcome about.

For fun, work along with me here. Think about an outcome you've wanted but just haven't been able to achieve and write it down below. Be as clear as possible and include as much detail as needed to describe how it looks, feels, smells, etc.:

To help you out, here are 12 of the major areas of your life that may be impacted by your outcome:

1. Family and Relationships
2. Career
3. Finances/Income
4. Health, Fitness and Well-Being
5. Spirituality and Faith
6. Home Environment
7. Hobbies or Volunteer Work
8. Leisure and Fun
9. Sex and Intimacy
10. Relationship to Yourself (Self Esteem, Self Confidence)
11. Relationship to Making a Difference in The World
12. Plans for the Future or Retirement

## STEP 2: WHAT DO YOU BELIEVE?

**[Luke:]** "I can't believe it."

**[Yoda:]** "That is why you fail."

So now that you've established your outcome, your first challenge comes with believing that you can actually do it (in the case of this book, it's to double your profits within the next six months). Many people will get stuck here without even knowing it or acknowledging it.

We become what we think about. Every moment of every day our minds are creating thoughts - or repeating old ones. Sometimes this moves us forward; sometimes it holds us back.

Our thoughts create our beliefs. If you think your customers are cheap and difficult to work with, then you will create a belief that says customers are cheap and difficult. If that is what you believe, then that is what you will experience in your life.

If you believe that you are worth a maximum of $100,000 per year, then there is no way you will be able to get to $200,000 per year. If you believe that **$ [Fill in the blank]** is out of reach for you, then it will be.

You see, you will not - and cannot - increase your profits (or get anything else you truly desire) unless you absolutely believe in your heart, with every part of your being, that it is possible... *for you*.

In fact, you have to get yourself to EXPECT that it's going to happen. There is no other way. You cannot think and believe something is impossible and expect it to show up on your doorstep.

Many people will ask: "What if I can't, or don't believe?" This is a great question. When you stretch your desired outcomes to new heights, often times it will be hard to believe that it's possible.

I'll tell you what I believe the culprit is in most of these situations: the insidious three-letter word: "HOW?"

> HOW can I increase my profits when I'm having such a hard time generating leads?
>
> HOW can I take more time off when I can barely afford to pay myself?
>
> HOW can I be, do or have ______________[the thing you desire] if ________ [the thing you think is in the way]?

You see, when we set a large goal/outcome, our mind immediately wants to know "how." This is the worst question we can ask ourselves, because most of the time we have absolutely no idea how the thing we desire will come about. (By the way, back at Step 1 did you write down what your REAL desire was or did you write down what you thought *might* be possible? Just FYI, most people will do the latter. If you wrote your true desire, congratulations. If you did write down what you thought might be possible, don't worry; after reading this section you will hopefully go back and change it!).

When we allow the question of "how" to dominate our minds, it leads to all kinds of unproductive thoughts. Namely: doubt, uncertainty, worry and fear. Again, you cannot desire a thing, believe it is impossible to get and then expect it to show up on your doorstep.

Since the publishing of the first edition of this book, I've studied this subject much deeper than I had in previous years. I have come to recognize not only the power of belief - but maybe more importantly - the power of FAITH. And given the economic climate of the past few years, I felt it necessary to discuss this further - and in more depth - than in the previous edition.

First, I recognize that the word "Faith" often carries with it a religious implication and it'll turn some people off. BUT, I know of no success system that does not also include the power of FAITH. Here is a definition of faith that I like: *"Faith is believing in things when common sense tells you not to."*

I can't know what your religious beliefs are, nor does it matter to me. For our purposes here, there are really 2 kinds of faith that successful people possess. First, is the faith and confidence they have in themselves (think Donald Trump). Second, is the faith and confidence they have in a higher power. Some call this power God (as I do); some call it the Universe, the Source, Infinite Intelligence and so on. It really doesn't matter what you call it, but successful people - regardless of profession - generally possess a higher level of faith and self confidence than the ordinary person (this has been very well documented).

With that said, let's get back to this question of "how". First, you should know that I don't believe in coincidences or luck (in the traditional sense - I believe we create what looks to the uninitiated as luck). I also don't believe in "manifesting" money and Porsches sitting under a tree meditating.

Here's what I've noticed... the more we focus on trying to figure out "how" we will be, do or have our outcome, the harder it will be to get what we want.

Yes, I know it sounds counterproductive, especially when the self-help people are telling you to make lists and just keep working the plan. But trust me... it's true. (In fact, don't trust me alone - look back on your life, you'll also know this to be true.)

Think about this for a minute.

Think about something great that happened in your life. Maybe how you met your spouse. How you started your business. How you bought your first house. How you met someone that helped you in some way. Did it come about because you had figured out every detail of how it was going to happen?

I couldn't have figured out how to have made all the best things that have happened to me beforehand - both personally and professionally - not in a million years... and I doubt you could have either.

In the same way, you can't exactly figure out how your future outcomes will come about either. In fact, I've come to believe that it's not my job to figure it out. My job is only to decide on what I want, believe it's possible for me, expect it to show up and then move forward, take ACTION!

You see, I'm convinced (again, because of experience and study) that when you set your intention for an outcome - no matter how big or small - and you move toward it, the Universe begins to reshape itself so it can deliver to you what you desire.

**Yes, I know how that sounds.**

But, think about it, this is what's happening at every moment of your life. Everything you think about, believe in and expect is constantly being delivered to you. What you focus on expands. So if you think about having a thriving, successful business - despite what's happening with the economy - and you believe that is possible for you, and act accordingly, then you will have that. Conversely, if you listen to the doom and gloom, and let it occupy your thoughts, beliefs and expectations, then you will suffer. And it's up to you to decide. To decide whether you will be living a dream... or living a nightmare.

> *"Men often become what they believe themselves to be. If I believe I cannot do something, it makes me incapable of doing it. But when I believe I can, then I acquire the ability to do it even if I didn't have it in the beginning."*
>
> **- Mahatma Ghandi**

I have seen a lot of things that look like luck or coincidence but upon closer study were this phenomenon in action.

Once you've taken your first step, the next step you need to take will be revealed to you. Read that again: *your next step will be revealed to you.*

When that step (sometimes leap - "leap of faith") is revealed to you, it will depend on your commitment, belief and faith whether or not you take that step (or leap). By the way, I believe this book, ending up in your hands at this moment of your life, could be (likely is) one of the next steps of your journey.

The truth is that you only need to take the NEXT step... not the next six, just the next ONE. That's why the how is unimportant.

## STEP 3: ARE YOU SUFFICIENTLY MOTIVATED?

*"Desire is the starting point of all achievement, not a hope, not a wish, but a keen pulsating desire which transcends everything."*
***Napoleon Hill***

At the start of this chapter I said: "We will not get what we want until something shakes us up with such emotional intensity, with such conviction and with such passion that we have to make it happen."

Imagine for a minute that I walked into your business today, put a gun to your head and told you that if you didn't increase your profits by the end of the week, I would come back and shoot you dead Friday night! To take this example to the next level, imagine that now I told you I had your spouse and children locked in a basement somewhere and the only way I would let you have them back is if you doubled your profits by the end of the month.

Would you get it done? Of course you would. Why? Because you would do whatever it took. You would have a clear outcome, you would have emotional intensity. And you would be committed!

Admittedly this is a horrible example, BUT how did you feel when reading that? Did you have emotional intensity? Did I give you a strong reason that you HAD to succeed or else the consequences would be catastrophic?

You see, part of the reason why we don't reach our goals or get what we truly want is because: a) we don't have a clear picture of the outcome; and b) we don't have enough motivation to do the things we have to do and be what we have to be. I call this having a "strong why". And the stronger the "WHY", the greater your chances of achieving the outcome.

In the admittedly frightening example above, you had the ultimate in motivation. You couldn't fail. You would have done anything to accomplish the goal.

My point with the example is that if you aren't sufficiently motivated, you will not be able to make the commitment (Step 4) necessary to achieve your desired outcome. But I'm not talking about the 'rah-rah' external motivation that you get from a tape or seminar; that's all temporary and rarely works.

Real motivation comes from a desire within. In the classic book *Think and Grow Rich*, Napoleon Hill calls it a "burning desire". You must want the outcome so strongly that you will endure any pain, any sacrifice and do any job that is required to have it. It's this intense desire that keeps people working all hours, up early, late to bed. The desire dominates your conversation, your thinking and your actions.

Here is what the great Muhammad Ali said:

> "Champions aren't made in the gyms. Champions are made from something they have deep inside them: a desire; a dream; a vision. They have to have last-minute stamina, they have to be a little faster, and they have to have the skill and the will. But the will must be stronger than the skill."

Only you can know if you are sufficiently motivated to achieve your desired outcome; but without that motivation...without that desire... you will never be able to get to Step 4, which is the most important component of achieving any outcome.

So here's another exercise for you. Use the space below to answer some of the questions presented here.

Once you've decided on the outcome you want, it's time to really understand why you want it. You accomplish this by digging deep and realizing how your life will be different as a result of that outcome. The best way I have found to do this is to ask yourself:

> Who or what will I BE that is different from who or what I am today?
>
> What will I DO differently than I do today?
>
> What will I HAVE that is different than what I have today?"

Take a minute on the next page to answer these questions .

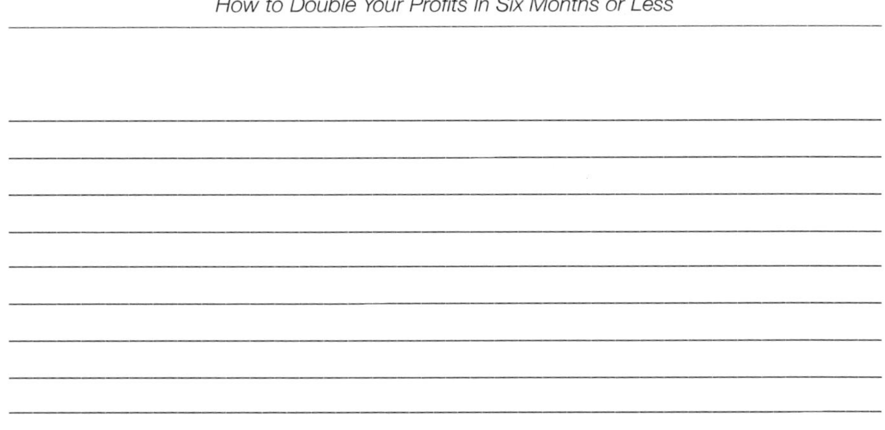

It is so much easier to reach the outcome if you know the REAL reasons why you want it!

## STEP 4: WHAT IS YOUR LEVEL OF COMMITMENT?

*"Losers make promises they often break.*
*Winners make commitments they always keep."*
**- Denis Waitley**

So let's stop here for a minute and look at what we've got so far. We should have an outcome we desire. We should believe it is possible for us. We should understand why we want it and have attached emotional intensity or a burning desire for the outcome.

Now, with all of those in place you'd think we're well on our way to having it all... but, not quite. We still have one more critical piece of the puzzle before we can actually get moving.

And that is **commitment**.

To succeed as an entrepreneur requires decision, determination and total, unwavering commitment.

How committed are you to have that successful, profitable business that funds your lifestyle? How strong is your commitment to travel the world or fully fund your children's education? How bad do you want to get to your healthy weight?

What are you willing to do to be able to take regular vacations from the office? How badly do you want to have the peace of mind that comes from having 12 months, 24 months or 60 months' of living expenses in an account, available to you at any given moment?

Ultimately, I don't believe we get what we want; we only get what we commit to. When you set a new direction for your life... when you desire a different outcome... you are going to be confronted by challenges at every turn.

Your motivation, strength of will and determination to succeed will be challenged every day. You will feel like giving up... you will feel frustration... you may start to lose faith and confidence in yourself... you may even suffer what looks like failure or defeat. (I haven't met or studied many successful people who haven't dealt with their share of challenges, disappointment and failure... or in many cases, even financial ruin.) That may be part of the process. I know it has been for me. But it's in those times - the times your faith is tested - when you must muster up the courage to keep pressing forward. This is where your commitment to your outcome - to a better business and a better life - will keep you going.

Napoleon Hill said, "Before success comes in any man's life, he's sure to meet with much temporary defeat and perhaps some failures. When defeat overtakes a man, the easiest and the most logical thing to do is to quit. That's exactly what the majority of men do."

When working privately with clients, we gauge the level of commitment to every action and outcome. We do this because while you can say that you are committed to the outcome, you also have to be committed to the actions necessary to achieve it. Only those actions that you commit to will ever come about. If your commitment isn't strong enough, you will not persist until the outcome is achieved. You will give up. Look around, the masses give up. They write off their desire as an impossible dream, especially in times like these. They let others tell them what is possible. And unfortunately they often times are so focused on just surviving that they forget to live. But this is not so for the successful man or woman... no, they keep pressing forward.

To me, this conversation is the missing ingredient in most goal-setting/achievement programs. If you look at any successful person, you will see this unwavering commitment to the end result. A willingness to do whatever it takes. I have learned that we will never get that outcome we want if we aren't absolutely committed to doing whatever must be done (ethical and legal of course) to get it.

## STEP 5: CREATING YOUR GAME PLAN

*"Some people dream of success...*
*while others wake up and work hard at it "*

We know that if we continue doing the same things over and over, we will continue to get the same results. So we have to come up with a new set of actions, habits and behaviors.

Throughout this book we'll take you through a number of exercises designed to help you develop a game plan, complete with a list of action items that you'll need to complete to achieve your desired result. But don't worry if you don't feel like you aren't getting everything you need or if all you can think about are obstacles. Many people get hung up here; often times we don't get started because we don't know what to do or how to do it. Do the exercises in this book, and by the end you will not only have enough raw material to begin formulating your game plan but you will have already started taking the actions necessary to bring about results.

## STEP 6: TAKE ACTION!

*"I hated every minute of training, but I said, Don't quit. Suffer now*
*and live the rest of your life as a champion."*
**- Muhammad Ali**

A famous sales trainer named Red Motley said: "nothing happens until somebody sells something"! You can also say: "nothing happens until you do something". If you look at any successful person or company, you will find massive, focused action behind the outcome.

We cannot get our desired outcome without movement... without execution... without ACTION!

Too many business owners passively wait for something to happen in their business, rather than proactively doing something to make something happen.

I have always been a believer that action (or inaction), causes reaction. If you take action to increase your profits, then that is what will happen. This book will provide you with many action steps you can immediately begin taking to cause the reaction of increased profits. But this formula works in the opposite direction - your inaction will also cause a reaction, but not a good one.

Sometimes the necessary actions will not be easy and they may require pain and sacrifice. But again, how strong is your "why"? How committed are you to the result or outcome? Is it merely a hope, a wish, a fantasy... or is it something you are truly committed to having, being or doing?

In Step 2 we talked about taking the first step. Some people will think the first step is merely bringing in someone like me to create a map of where to take the business. I can come up with 8 ways or 27 ways to increase your profits, but it will be up to you to take the first action. So in Section 4 I'll introduce you to a tool that will help you take your first steps to take ACTION... and action with a plan.

## STEP 7: MEASURE AND EVALUATE YOUR RESULTS

*"Never, never, never, never give up."*
**- Winston Churchill**

Now that you've taken ACTION you will start to see results. You will constantly need to monitor your results to make sure you stay on track. If you are off track, you'll need to make the required adjustments. If certain commitments or actions aren't working for you, go back and find alternatives.

As you delve deeper into achieving your outcome, you will notice something interesting start to happen. Your outcome and your pursuit of it will produce 'by-products.' These by-products will often be better than the actual outcome you were working toward. Be on the lookout for them; don't let them pass you by.

Of course once you've achieved your result, it's time for you to go back and start the process over again with new outcomes. The more you practice, the more you'll achieve.

Finally, be grateful in advance for the outcome. Be grateful for what that outcome will do for your business, for your family, for you.

**A CONTRARY THOUGHT**

Throughout this process you may find that you really don't want the outcome as much as you thought you did or that it wasn't important enough to you.

I am going to make a comment here that wouldn't be very popular with most of the self-help gurus, here it is:

> When you realize you really don't want the outcome as much as you thought you did - or that it wasn't important enough to you - let it go!

That's right, let it go and move on. If you have to adjust the outcome, do so; if you have to kill it completely, do it. But don't beat yourself up or destroy your self-image or self-worth by attaching labels to yourself because you didn't achieve the outcome. Accept the fact that at this point that outcome is just not important enough to you. Accept yourself for who you are. Accept the consequences that come with that choice and love and appreciate who you are WITHOUT that result.

Express your gratitude with total faith and expectancy as if the outcome has already happened. There is no more powerful process for getting what you want.

Now I realize for some this is all a little bit "out there"; it used to be for me too. I would suggest devoting some time to studying this subject. The great Jim Rohn said, **"Work harder on yourself than on your business."** I take that advice to heart, and do my best to practice it every day.

I'll finish this section with a quote about commitment that I love:

"Until one is committed, there is hesitancy, the chance to draw back, always ineffectiveness. Concerning all acts of initiative and creation, there is one elementary Truth, the ignorance of which kills countless ideas and splendid plans: that the moment one commits oneself, then Providence moves, too. All sorts of things occur to help one that would never otherwise have occurred. A whole stream of events issues from the decision, raising in ones favor all manner of unforeseen incidents and meetings and material assistance, which no man could have come his way."

**- W.H. Murray**

# CHAPTER 2

## To Double Your Profits, You've Got to Understand the Business You Are Really In...

Like me, when you first went into business or sales (whether working for yourself or someone else), you probably thought "technical" knowledge about your product or service was all you really needed to be successful.

You thought that if you became the "best" carpet cleaner, CPA, dry cleaner, auto mechanic ____________ [fill in the blank with your profession], that alone would be enough to make you successful. If you are in the restaurant business, you probably thought that if your food was better than everyone else's, that would make you successful.

You thought that because of your expertise and knowledge, customers would seek you out when they heard how "good" you were.

So you set out to be really good...maybe great...maybe even "the best" in your field. You read books, attended conferences and worked tirelessly every day to get better and better at doing "the thing" in your business.

And you honestly believed that if you or your company really did what you do better than the next guy, the world would pay attention, beat a path to your door and support you in style for the rest of your days!

But something happened that you didn't expect.

Even though you have a great business - and DO have the best products or services - people haven't beaten a path to your door! In fact, the hardest thing about being in business IS getting people to buy from you!

Am I right?

Let's speak candidly.

I know what's wrong. I know why you don't sell as much as you could. I know why you don't make the kind of money you deserve to make.

And what I'm going to share with you is based on years of experience and results. But before I share it with you, let me tell you a quick personal story about my first business.

My first business was a carpet dyeing and cleaning business. I knew the carpet cleaning business fairly well because a friend of a friend, John, was already in the carpet cleaning business.

When I entered the business, my plan was to do everything myself the first year, including the actual carpet dyeing and cleaning work. I would then work myself "off the truck" as quickly as possible.

So I hit the streets and went looking for customers (because we all know sitting by the phone waiting for it to ring doesn't always work!). One customer led to another and pretty soon I was busy every day doing carpet cleaning work...hard, back-breaking carpet cleaning work.

Now here is the interesting part. I was doing the same level of business - after just a few months - as John was doing after 7 years. Within 3 years of starting that business, I had a thriving, very profitable business with 5 trucks, an office and - most importantly - after the first year, I never did any more of the back-breaking work, ever!

I'll spare you the details of the rest of my story, but let me make my point. After 10 years, John was still doing the same level of revenue as he had always done; and to make matters worse, he was still "on the truck, pushing the wand" EVERY DAY!

What was the difference?

Obviously the difference was focus. Specifically - as business owners - which area(s) did each of us focus our time and energy on?

My focus was on building a profitable and valuable business; his focus was to be a great cleaner of carpet... big difference.

But looking back, we both got what we focused on. I said it back then, and I'll say it now: "John was THE BEST cleaner of carpet around... PERIOD!" I knew the other guys in our market and I knew him; he was - without question - technically the best at getting carpets clean.

So why am I telling you this story?

Because my story illustrates an important point - being the best doer or maker of your "thing" does not guarantee your success.

You may be the best there is at what you do; but it's just not good enough to be the best doctor, the best chef, the best plumber, or the best furniture dealer around. If it were, you'd be getting all of the business and profits you could handle, wouldn't you?

I know this statement upsets some people. That's really not my intent. But the fact is - and it's a very important fact that every business person must grasp - you're not in the business you think you're in.

## SHIFTING FROM THE DOER OF "THE THING" TO...

As I said, being the best doer of your "thing" does not guarantee your success. In fact, I believe that the doing or making of your "thing" is the least profitable use of your time. I'll take it one step further by saying that "the doing or making of your 'thing' is the least profitable skill you possess".

If it truly is your desire to double (or substantially increase) your profits, you must break away from the desire to be the best doer or maker of your product or service, and become the best marketer of your product or service.

Here is an undeniable truth: The real money is not in the doing of "the thing,", but rather in the marketing of the thing.

This means you have to make an important shift in your thinking about the business you are in. It means you must accept the fact that you are no longer a dry cleaner, doctor, computer repairman, plumber or consultant.

If you truly want to double (or substantially increase) your profits, you must now become a...

## MARKETER OF YOUR PRODUCTS AND SERVICES!

Marketing is about **understanding customers** and finding ways to provide them products or services they want and need.

I tell my clients we're all in the same business - we're in the customer business. Specifically, we're in the business of creating, keeping and multiplying customers. And this is done with effective marketing.

This is true without exception - no matter what you sell, how you sell it, or who you sell it to - if you want to make more money, you must become a marketer first, and a dry cleaner, doctor, computer repairman, plumber, consultant, or whatever, second.

In the personal example I gave you above, I shifted away from being the doer of cleaning carpets to the marketer of carpet cleaning, dyeing and restoration services.

I was fortunate enough to discover early on that marketing is the ultimate form of business leverage, and if you do it right, it can make you rich!

The acceptance of your role as marketer is essential. Until you do this, you'll never make the kind of money you want to make. Let's face it, in any business - and yours is no different - the best marketer wins!

Is this rule breakable or flexible in any way? No! Why not? Because it's true...it's always been true...and always will be true. He or she who markets best, makes more money.

To help you with this concept, let me give you an important piece of advice.

The number one mistake business owners make is that regardless of what they sell or what industry they are in, they think about themselves first... their needs... their wants... and their expectations.

They liken their customers, clients and patients to themselves, claiming that their customers are just like they are and base their decisions and actions on this absolutely false belief.

As a marketer of your product or service, it is your job to figure out what your customers' needs, wants and expectations are and then create a product, service, message and a company that appeals to them.

## HOW TO THINK LIKE A MARKETER

*"Remember that the people you address are selfish, as we all are. They care nothing about your interest or your profit. They seek service for themselves. Ignoring this fact is a common mistake and a costly mistake in advertising."*

I didn't write these words; they were written by Claude Hopkins in 1923. Although he has been dead for many years, Claude Hopkins is still considered (by those of us who know) to be one of the world's leading authorities on direct-response marketing.

To be a successful marketer (and successful business person), you MUST always be thinking of your customers first. The level of your income (up or down) will be in direct proportion to how effectively you can answer the following questions about your customers:

What are **their** needs, **their** wants, and **their** expectations?

What keeps them awake at night?

What problem does your product or service solve for them?

What are the benefits (not to be mistaken with features) of your product or service?

If you want to break free and break through to the next level of success and profitability, you must acknowledge that you are in business to solve a problem or problems for your clients. You must also understand that they are selfish. They are buying your product or service for ***their*** satisfaction, not yours.

Once you understand this concept, you will be the one seller of your product or service in your market that truly understands the needs of their clients. By properly designing your business and communicating your solutions in an effective way, prospective clients will quickly recognize that you are not only the best choice - but the **only & obvious** choice - for them to do business with.

Once they realize this, they will seek you out and approach your business ready to buy, without having to be "sold." They will be appreciative and loyal, and be happy to pay a premium price because you aren't just standing behind a register collecting money; you are solving their problems and making their lives better. And best of all, you will serve them so well that they will act as your unpaid sales force, telling the world how you are the best choice - the only choice - for solving their problem.

So now it's your turn to make a shift in your thinking. On the following page you'll find a fast and easy exercise called **Making The Shift**™. The goal of this simple exercise is to begin the process of turning yourself into a marketer of your product or service rather than the doer of your product or service.

Please, stop and do this exercise. There is the temptation to skip it to come back to it later... which you and I both know is not very likely. So, if you are serious about increasing your income and your business's profits you will stop now and spend some time with this exercise. It will look simple, even easy. However, I can assure you it is one of the most powerful in this book.

## EXERCISE #2A - MAKING THE SHIFT™
## PART 1

1) **"I am no longer a(n) ______________________________."**
**--Insert what you now do or make.--**

**Examples:**
"I am no longer an accountant."
"I am no longer a mechanic."
"I am no longer a chef."
"I am no longer the owner of a menswear (or other retail) store."

2) **"I am now a marketer of ______________ products/services."**

**Examples:**
"I am now a marketer of accounting services."
"I am now a marketer of auto repair services."
"I am now the marketer of a restaurant."
"I am now the marketer of a menswear store."

Use the space below to rewrite both sentences in their completed forms. When complete, it should look like this:

I AM NO LONGER A CARPET CLEANER. I AM NOW A MARKETER OF CARPET CLEANING, DYEING AND RESTORATION SERVICES.

______________________________________________________________

______________________________________________________________

______________________________________________________________

______________________________________________________________

______________________________________________________________

## EXERCISE #2A - MAKING THE SHIFT™
## PART 2

As a marketer of ______________________________________________,
what problem(s) does my product or service solve for my clients?

What are the benefit(s)* of my product or service for my clients?

How do I answer the most pressing question in my prospect's mind: "**What's in it for me?**"

______________________________________________

______________________________________________

______________________________________________

______________________________________________

______________________________________________

*Don't confuse features of your product or service with benefits. Features are characteristics of your product or service, the benefits are the advantages your features give your clients, for example:

| Feature | Benefit |
|---|---|
| 4 Auto Repair Bays | Fast service, no waiting |
| Truck-mounted cleaning machine | Deep-down clean carpet |
| Award-winning chef | Unique, daily specials |
| Shoe sizes from 3 – 15 | We'll have your size in stock |

# CHAPTER 3

## To Double Your Profits, You've Got To Understand What A Customer Really Is...

In the last chapter, I suggested that the only way to actually double your profits is to become a marketer of your product or service, rather than a doer or maker of your product or service.

So now that you are a marketer of your products and services, in this chapter we are going to go a step further and help you start thinking like a marketer.

If you are truly committed to doubling the profits of your business and getting everything from your business that you want, then you must change the way you view the people that patronize your business.

First, I'd like you to start thinking about how valuable your customers are to your business over the course of years rather than just what they purchase from you today. With my clients, I suggest they call the patrons of their business **clients** instead of customers.

Why the importance of a semantic change? To me, the word "customer" implies that the person just buys something from you once. But the word "client" implies a **relationship**. Clients are people you care about - people with whom you have a history. Clients regard you as more than a service provider—they see you as a partner in solving their problems and needs.

This is a simple - but powerful - distinction. To truly grow your business you've got to get away from transactions and get focused on relationships... especially in the "New Economy."

And by the way, this type of language is not limited to "professionals" like accountants, doctors or lawyers. Regardless of what kind of business you're in, if you want to grow this is the language to use when thinking about the people who give your business money.

Now that we're thinking about the people who give us money the right waylet's begin thinking like marketers. We'll start with our clients.

## THE MOST VALUABLE ASSET YOUR BUSINESS HAS

One of the biggest mistakes so many business owners make is that they spend way too much time, energy and resources ($$$) chasing after the next new customer to get the next transaction.

I'll be the first to admit that I've been guilty of this. In one of my businesses, over a 3-year period I spent over one million dollars in advertising to get NEW customers. And I hate to admit it, but all we looked at was how many transactions we were doing and how much money was going in the bank.

We didn't think about what our customers could (or would) be worth over the long haul; we only looked at what they were worth that minute, that week, that month. I knew better, but I still did it, and I know now that I paid the price in lost profits and lost business value. My justification for it (probably the same as yours): it was working at the time.

The problem with this thinking is that the real value, profit potential and long-term sustainability of your business is not in the transactions, but in the number of good quality, profitable client relationships your business builds and maintains.

## WELCOME TO THE CASH COW RANCH

Here is a great analogy to dr ive this point home. Now I'll warn you, some of you may not like this analogy and may not find it "proper" or "politically correct", but it is the most effective analogy I can use to make this point.Imagine that you and I are in the cattle business. We own the Cash Cow Ranch. On our ranch we have a herd of cows and our cows produce milk that we sell and convert into cash.

I think you'd agree that the success of our business depends on how effectively and profitably we produce and sell our milk.

I think you'd also agree that if we wanted to grow the Cash Cow Ranch business we'd have to always be figuring out how many cows we have to buy in order to produce the amount of milk we need to cover our overhead, and to make a profit.

Now as ranchers, wouldn't our profits be dependent on how often and how effectively our cows produced milk?

Of course they would. If our cows could produce milk (money, purchases and profits) three times a month, why would we settle for once per month?

As good ranchers, do you think that we would milk our cows just once, and then let them go? Of course not.

If we just let them go, we'd have to get new cows every day to keep up with our production, and that would kill our profits.

So we would probably nurture them, care for them and do whatever we could to protect our "cash cows" so that they could produce milk again tomorrow.

As the owners of this ranch, do you think we would feed and care for our cows so they'll be healthy??

Of course we would. We couldn't expect our cows to produce milk every day if we fed them only once in a while.

As the owners of this ranch, do you think we would install a fence around the ranch to keep the cattle in?

Of course we would, because left on their own the cows would probably wander off, get lost or make their way to another ranch, never to be seen or heard from again.

As the owners of this ranch, do you think we would constantly be on the lookout for any intruders who may harm or steal our cows?

Of course we would; our cows are valuable and we don't want anyone stealing or harming them.

Let's say that after working the ranch for a few years, we were ready to move on to something new, or we wanted to retire; wouldn't we decide to sell our ranch and get the maximum value for it?

Of course we would. Just imagine how excited a potential buyer would be when he saw that we had the healthiest, most effective milk-producing cows in all of town or in our state? Conversely, how would a potential buyer feel if we were buying new cows every day, feeding our existing cows every once in a while and our ranch didn't have a strong, sturdy fence up around it?

Now you may or may not like the analogy, but if you haven't figured it out, the cows are your clients and your business is the ranch. And just like a rancher that buys cows, you - as a business owner - are buying clients every day.

As the owner of a business, you have no more important job than to create new clients and then care for, nurture and protect your "herd" of existing clients. The better you care for and protect your clients, the more purchases they'll make from you, and the more purchases they make, the more profit you'll have to increase the size of your herd.

Now don't get me wrong... I absolutely believe you MUST constantly pursue new clients for your business. You must constantly add new clients to your herd; however, you cannot let that pursuit eat up all of your available resources for getting the most out of your current herd of clients.

So let me suggest a different way to view your relationship to client acquisition; this is one of the most important principles that you MUST walk away from this book with:

**You MUST Be Thinking Of Making The Sale To Get The Client (To Add To Your Herd), NOT Getting A Customer To Make A Sale.**

Let me say that again: "***You must make the sale to get the client***".

In fact, your real profits are rarely ever on the initial transaction; the real profits are in the relationship that you create with your herd of clients. The quality of that relationship will determine not only your level of profitability today, but also your future riches.

What do I mean by future riches?

A customer or client actually has at least 6 value factors... after the initial transaction. One of the most important is the marginal net value that that client can add to the value of your business. I do a lot of work with people who want to sell their businesses. Almost without fail, every one of us thinks our business is worth much more than it really is. All too often, I have to break the news to the business owner that his "baby" is worth far less than he thinks it is.

Don't make the mistake of thinking that the value of your business is based solely on financial statements, buildings, machinery, computers or other hard assets. A major reason that a business is not worth what the owner thinks it's worth is because after X number of years, the business is still chasing transactions.

If you want to get maximum value when you sell your business, demonstrate to the prospective buyer the quality of your relationship with your herd. Prove that you have meaningful, sustainable relationships that bring predictable, profitable, repeat transactions with a fraction of the effort and your business will be worth many times what you thought it was worth... AND it will be easier to sell.

Later in this book, I'm going to present a number of strategies and methods for developing sustainable, profitable relationships with your clients. But first, we need a powerful piece of information about your clients that most business owners completely ignore.

## UNDERSTANDING LPV - HOW MUCH IS A CLIENT WORTH TO YOUR BUSINESS?

One of the first things I want to know when consulting with a business owner is how much money a client is worth over the entire lifecycle of their relationship with the business. I call this "LPV" (Lifetime Profit Value of a Client) and every business has a unique number. Unfortunately, I will stump almost every client with this question.

The "LPV" number includes every transaction they'll make, up-sell/cross-sell opportunities, referral opportunities and ultimately, the marginal value they'll add when the business is sold.

Here are a couple of reasons why this number is so important:

First - as a consultant - without this number it's hard to decide what advice to dispense, what opportunities are available and which strategies will provide the fastest results. Also, until you know exactly what each new client is worth to your business, you won't know how much money you can spend in marketing to acquire (or buy) a new client.

Secondly, by understanding what each client is potentially worth to your business, you'll have a greater appreciation for him or her and do things a little differently when they walk in or call; you'll devise ways of maximizing that value.

In just a minute, I'm going to show you how to figure out LPV for your business. But first, let me give you a couple of personal, practical examples of why LPV is so important.

**Example 1: Large-transaction business** - A few years ago, my wife and I leased a Cadillac Escalade. In the 3 years we had that vehicle, I did not hear from the dealership, not even once... no mail, no phone calls, no invitation to look at the new models...zilch...nada... NOTHING.

The car dealer is so busy thinking about the next big "deal" that once he's done with you, you become a statistic... nothing more than a sale or a number on a board and your file is buried with the rest of the statistics.

Running just a quick calculation, I estimate my potential worth to this Cadillac dealer (or any high-line car dealer) to be close to $1,000,000 (one million dollars)!

How do I get to such a big number? Think about it... I've already demonstrated a willingness and desire to replace a vehicle after 3 years. Given the potential that I'll be buying cars for at least another 30 years - and hopefully buying expensive cars - that alone is a minimum of ten vehicles at $50k to $80k per vehicle. Next, you have to factor in that each car will require financing, add-ons and service (the real money-makers for a dealership).

But wait... what about my wife? You don't think she'll let me have a nice car while she drives a Yugo... isn't she going to need a car every three years also?

Add this up and we're well over a million bucks in my lifetime.

The amazing thing about this is that it doesn't include all of my friends, neighbors and relatives who I could potentially refer, or the marginal value my business will add to the value of their business should they sell it! It also doesn't include the fact that over those 30 years, my kids might also need a car, and they may want one of that same dealer's new or used cars.

**Example 2: Small-transaction business** - There are a number of restaurants near my office where I eat lunch nearly every day. I walk in, place my order and pay the bill. Do I like the food? Sure. Do I like the service? Sure. But do they ever try to get my contact information so they can offer me special incentives to come back even more often? Never! When was the last time a restaurant even attempted to get your contact information so they could invite you back? My guess is never!

Let's review the same LPV (lifetime profit value) of a customer process. I eat lunch at these places at least 3 times per week, at least 40 weeks per year.

If the average lunch costs $8 (a bargain these days), I spend at least $1,000 (40 weeks X 3 days/week = 120 lunches X $8 = $960) on lunch in a year (and you could easily double that to $2,000 because I rarely eat alone). Now, let's add in one more factor... time. Chances are good my business will be in the same general area at least for the next 2 or 3 years.

So even if we limited my potential lifetime value to just 3 years, I'm easily worth $6,000. Now, I'm not suggesting they'll get my full $2,000 per year, but they could get a good percentage of it.

But the restaurant owner is so "busy" with the next order that they fail to consider how they can create a regular stream of diners so they can almost predict how many people will eat in their restaurant every day.

So here is the question... if you were the owner of a car dealership, and I bought a car from you - knowing what you know now - do you think you would treat our relationship in a very different way?

Are you starting to understand how powerful this concept is?

Regardless of the type of business you are in, if you think that the person who comes into your business today is worth a measly $8 (restaurant example), then it doesn't matter how you treat him. It doesn't matter how good the sandwich is or how good his experience is with your store, your staff or with you, because you know you're going to get the $8 today. BUT you also have to realize that more than likely that's all you're going to get.

Incidentally, as we all know the "Great Recession" decimated thousands of businesses - large and small alike - in almost every industry. Think about the businesses in your community that were hit hardest and have shut their doors or are on life support. How many once-thriving car dealers are gone? How many once "hot" restaurants are now gone? Do you think they understood this concept? HINT: If they did they'd still be around!

There's an old saying that goes: "Do what you've always done and get what you've always got." My good friend and mentor, Martin Howey, showed me that that's not necessarily true. In fact, it's dangerous. He says: "Do what you've always done and you'll get less than you've always got."

Here's how he explains it:

Let's say that you own ABC Widgets and I own XYZ Widgets, and we are the only 2 sellers of widgets in our town. Let's assume that you get exactly 50% of the total sales in our market and I get the other 50%. For years, we've been going along, you getting your share, and me getting mine. We've both comfortably assumed that if we kept doing the same things... we'll keep getting the same results, and for years we've been right

But this year, your daughter is going off to college, and you've discovered golf. Let's also say that your landlord decides it's time to increase your rent... substantially. You know that this year you have to make more money. So you make the decision to grow your business. You attend seminars; you pick up books like this one. You start to implement the strategies you're learning and your business starts to grow.

I on the other hand, continue doing the same things I've always done, assuming I'll continue getting the same results. After a few months I start to realize that sales are down and profits are way down. I don't have to finish the story because I think you know where it ends..

The point is - how many business owners just keep doing the same things and hoping for the same results? Worse, how many are doing the same things and hoping for different results (more sales, more profits, etc.)? My bet would be most of your competitors - which by the way, gives you an extraordinary strategic advantage!

Much of what you'll learn throughout this book will affect the lifetime profit value of your clients in a very positive way. <u>If you get nothing else from this book, let it be this</u>: **you can no longer afford to ignore the <u>total</u> potential value your best customers/clients/ patients.**

Now let's do a little math and get your LPV number. For our purposes here we are going to do a basic LPV calculation.

## Exercise 3a
## WHAT IS YOUR LPV?

| BASIC LPV CALCULATOR | | |
|---|---|---|
| Fill in the blanks below (using the numbers from your business), to learn what each client is actually worth to you and your business right now. | | |
| Average Sale= | **A** | $ |
| Average number of times a client purchases from your business in a year = | **B** | |
| Average number of years a client buys from you = | **C** | |
| Gross Sales per year, per client (A x B) = | **D** | $ |
| Total Lifetime Profit Value (D x C) = | **E** | $ |

**Profit Resource**

You will find a basic version of the Lifetime Profit Value calculator at: www.DoubleYourProfitBook.com for your use.

# CHAPTER 4

## To Double Your Profits, You've Got To Understand The 3 Fundamental Ways To Multiply Profits

To complete this first section, there is one more thing we need to know before moving on to the actual strategies we'll use for doubling your profits. And that is the three fundamental ways to grow your business:

1. **Increase The Number Of New Clients**

2. **Increase The Average Transaction Value Of Each Client**

3. **Increase The Number Of Times Each Client Returns And Buys Again**

You see, to grow your business and to multiply profits we have to understand the basic, fundamental ways it will happen. As you'll see in a minute, any increase in your top-line sales will come from doing one of these three things.

(Incidentally, for obvious reasons I am not offering strategies on increasing profits by cost cutting, implementing efficiencies, etc. The goal of this book is to show you how to <u>grow</u> the sales and profits of your business.)

Let's dig deeper into each of the three ways to grow your business:

## 1. INCREASE THE NUMBER OF CLIENTS

Increasing the number of clients is an obvious way to grow your business. If we currently serve 100 clients a month, adding 20 new clients will theoretically increase sales by 20%.

In Section 3 we'll discuss 4 strategies for increasing the number of new clients who come into your business. Implement those strategies and you will have fulfilled the number one requirement for growing your business.

## 2. INCREASE THE AVERAGE TRANSACTION VALUE EACH TIME A CUSTOMER BUYS

Every business has an average transaction value. Each time a client buys something from you, they spend a certain dollar amount. To increase the average spent, you need to increase the amount they spend each time you deal with them.

For example, a restaurant may increase their average transaction value by selling (yes, I used the word "selling") appetizers or desserts. They could raise their prices by 15%. If they sell wine, they could sell (there is that word again) and upgrade to a more expensive wine. If they are a fast-food restaurant, they could ask: "Would you like fries with that?" or "Would you like to super-size your order?"

There are many strategies you can execute to increase this number; in this book we'll discuss two. In *Chapter 7*, we'll discuss how we can get your customer to spend a little (or a lot) more each time they buy, and in *Chapter 8*, we'll talk about optimizing your prices.

## 3. INCREASE THE NUMBER OF TIMES YOUR CLIENT RETURNS AND BUYS AGAIN (OR BRINGS OTHERS - REFERRALS)

Most businesses do a very poor job of proactively getting their clients to come back and purchase more often and an even worse job of getting those clients to make referrals.

What would happen if you increased the frequency of purchase in your business? We'll discuss this in more detail in *Chapter 6*. But this is one of the most powerful ways to grow your business and is horribly underutilized by almost every business on the planet (okay, that might be a bit dramatic, but it's close).

**$$**

Before getting into the specific strategies we are going to use to grow your profits, I want to show you - on paper - EXACTLY HOW you are going to double (or significantly increase) your profits. To do this, I'll introduce you to a powerful tool I've developed called **The Profit Blaster Matrix™**.

When working with a client, I have to know all of the numbers that affect a business's sales and profits. For example: how many leads the business generates, or how many people walk into the store or restaurant on a given day, week or month. How many of those leads, visitors, guests or shoppers turn into a paying customer? How much do they spend on average? How many of your customers are repeat purchasers? How many referrals do you get? The list goes on, but I think you get the point.

The next step is to look at the areas where there are opportunities for immediate improvements. Once we've determined the best opportunities, I like to use the Profit Blaster Matrix™ to estimate the sales/profit increases we might generate by executing our business-building strategies within any of the areas of opportunity.

On the following pages you'll see the basic Profit Blaster at work. At the end of the chapter I'll give you access to your own copy of this powerful tool so you can use it for your business.

To demonstrate how The Profit Blaster Matrix™ works, I'll use a fictional service business. The business currently generates about $750,000 in annual revenue and has a 50% gross margin.

NOTE: I use gross profit margin in these examples. As a reminder, gross profit is what is left after your "hard" (or direct) costs for providing your service or product. This should not be confused with net profit, which is what's left over after every expense.

STEP 1: Our first step is to establish our baseline, which is essentially where we are right now. We start by entering the number of clients (750) the business services in a year.

Next, we'll enter the average transaction value ($500); this is the average amount a customer spends at each transaction.

Next, we'll enter the average number of purchases (2) a client will make in a year. And finally, we'll enter the gross profit percentage (50%) the business currently generates. This gives us our starting point of $750,000 in revenue and $375,000 in gross profit.

What the Profit Blaster tool allows us to do is determine how small, incremental improvements to the number of clients, average transaction value and average number of purchases will affect the sales and profits of the business. The way we'll do this is by "tweaking" our numbers to see what effect it will have on our sales and profits.

FIT BLASTER MATRIX™

| A | NUMBER OF CLIENTS | AVERAGE TRANSACTION VALUE | AVERAGE # OF PURCHASES | SALES | GROSS PROFIT | 50% |
|---|---|---|---|---|---|---|
| ERS | 750 | $ 500 | 2.0 | $750,000 | $375,000 | |

**B** STEP 2: We'll make a few "tweaks" to each of the numbers to estimate the change in revenue and profit. For our purposes, I'll use some fairly conservative numbers.

THE PROFIT BLASTER MATRIX™

| | NUMBER OF CLIENTS | AVERAGE TRANSACTION VALUE | AVERAGE # OF PURCHASES | SAL |
|---|---|---|---|---|
| CURRENT NUMBERS | 750 | $ 500 | 2.0 | $750, |
| INCREASE NUMBER OF CLIENT **B** | 825 | $ 500 | 2.0 | $825, |
| INCREASE AVERAGE TRANSACTION VALUE | 825 | $ 525 | 2.0 | $866, |
| INCREASE AVERAGE # OF PURCHASES | 825 | $ 525 | 2.5 | $1,08 |

**C** In our example, the first area we are going to work on improving is in the number of clients. If we increase the average number of customers by 10% (about 6 new clients per month), that will give us 75 new customers for a new total of 825 clients. This small change (for our purposes here I'm going to use very conservative improvement numbers) adds $75,000 to our revenue and potentially $37,500 to our bottom line, depending on the acquisition cost of those 75 customers. Keep in mind that we don't necessarily have to get more leads or do more advertising to get to this number - we can achieve this any number of ways, including improvement of our sales conversion ratio.

NOTE: As you change each variable, the Matrix will adjust the numbers to reflect the new results.

BLASTER MATRIX™

| | NUMBER OF CLIENTS | AVERAGE TRANSACTION VALUE | AVERAGE # OF PURCHASES | SALES | GROSS PROFIT | 50% | |
|---|---|---|---|---|---|---|---|
| C | 750 | $ 500 | 2.0 | $750,000 | $375,000 | | |
| LIENTS | 825 | $ 500 | 2.0 | $825,000 | $412,500 | $37,500 | 110% |
| NSACTION VALUE | 825 | $ 525 | 2.0 | $866,250 | $433,125 | $58,125 | |

Next, we look at the average transaction value. Let's say we improve that number by a minimal 5% (from $500 to $525); the effect it will have is increasing our revenue by $37,500 and our gross profit by $18,750.

Lastly, we look at the frequency of purchase. If we can improve the frequency of purchase from 2 times per year to an average of 2.5 times per year, that minor improvement would result in a revenue increase of $187,500 and a gross profit contribution of $93,750!

You'll notice as you use the Matrix that as you change each area it will give you the result with the previous change, meaning simultaneous changes. As a consultant, I will generally want to work in at least 2 areas simultaneously, to get the fastest results. Take a

**Incremental v. Simultaneous Implementation**

An important word about implementation. If you want speed... if you want to double your profits quick... then you've got to become a simultaneous implementer. Most people will take one area and work on for months tinkering here, tinkering there. In today's world there's no shortage of ideas or opportunities. But, the money will always flow to the implementer - to the person that's get's sh*t **done**. So, I would suggest executing strategies in 2 - or even all 3 - areas at once.

look at the table below to see the results we could expect if we were to implement in 2 areas at once.

| The Effects of 2 Simultaneous Changes | | | |
|---|---|---|---|
| | Revenue Change | Gross Profit $ Change | Gross Profit % Increase |
| Increase Number of Clients & Transaction Size ONLY | **$ 116,250** | **$ 58,125** | **15.5%** |
| Increase Number of Clients and Frequency of Purchase ONLY | **$ 281,250** | **$ 140,625** | **37.5%** |
| Increase Transaction Size and Frequency of Purchase ONLY | **$ 234,375** | **$ 117,188** | **31.2%** |

Notice that the last example adds $117,188 in gross profit and doesn't require adding any new clients!

Now the real results come when you make improvements in all 3 areas at once. Take a look at what happens.

| | | | | | | |
|---|---|---|---|---|---|---|
| | 750 | $ 500 | 2.0 | $750,000 | $375,000 | |
| CLIENTS | 825 | $ 500 | 2.0 | $825,000 | $412,500 | $37,500 |
| NSACTION VALUE | 825 | $ 525 | 2.0 | $866,250 | $433,125 | $58,125 |
| F PURCHASES | 825 | $ 525 | 2.5 | $1,082,813 | $541,406 | $166,406 |
| | | | GROSS SALES DIFFERENCE | $332,813 | | |

You get a revenue increase of 44% - or $332,813 - and a gross profit increase of...

**$166,406**

That's not revenue; that's **gross profit contribution**!

I think you'll agree that the proposed changes – 75 new clients, 10% increase in the average purchase size, and an increase in frequency of average purchase from 2 times to 2.5 times – over the course of a year is very conservative.

Depending on the type of business, this 44% increase in gross profit could easily add over $100,000 in additional net profits to the owner. You see, there's no magic here... there's no sleight of hand. We're talking basic business-building strategies. And as a marketer of your products and services... this is they type of work you can now engage in and take your profits through the roof!

So now we're ready to move on to Section 2 where you'll discover the actual strategies and tactics you'll use in your business to: a) increase the number of clients who buy from you; b) increase the amount of each transaction; and c) increase the number of times they purchase from you.

**Profit Resource**

Now that you know the top 3 ways to grow your revenues and profits, let's see how making small changes/improvements - using the strategies in sections 2 and 3 of this book - will MULTIPLY your profits!

You will find a basic version of The Profit Blaster Matrix™ at: www.DoubleYourProfitBook.com for your use.

# SECTION TWO

## UNCOVERING THE HIDDEN RICHES LYING DORMANT AND NEGLECTED WITHIN YOUR BUSINESS

*"A 'normal' small business can only yield a 'normal' small business income. To earn an extraordinary income, you must develop an extraordinary business!"*

Dan S. Kennedy
Dan Kennedy's Eternal Truth #17

# CHAPTER 5

## Double Your Profits STRATEGY #1: Fencing In Your Herd

To double your business's profits, make it immune to competition and make it a valuable, sustainable **asset** that you can rely on, you must have a system in place that maximizes the profit potential of every new client you acquire. And that system must have one singular purpose: to turn that one-time transaction into a long-term, profitable ***relationship***.

In the last chapter we discussed that your most profitable assets are your current and former clients. However, most business owners are always so busy trying to chase after the next new customer that they completely neglect the ones they already have.

Allow me to take us back to the Cash Cow Ranch for a minute and ask you a question: "As the owner of the Cash Cow Ranch, how would you sleep at night if you didn't have a good, solid fence around your herd of cows?"

I don't know about you... but I wouldn't sleep very well.

Why?

I'd be afraid of waking up in the morning to find that some (or all) of my cows were missing!

Yet, isn't this what business owners do every day? We go to sleep without a strong, solid fence around our herd of clients and we hope that when we wake up in the morning they'll all still be there. And even worse, we naively assume that they are going to come back to our business and give us more money!

So many business owners mistakenly believe that if they give their clients great service, prepare great food, provide the "best" products... their herd of clients is safe from being snatched away by their competitors.

They mistakenly believe that once someone buys their product or service, they are now somehow magically loyal to their business and will return every time they need their product or service. I'm sorry to be the one to tell you... this couldn't be further from the truth.

Here is the sad truth: depending on your type of business, anywhere from 12 seconds to 12 hours to 12 days after the transaction has occurred, that person who bought from you, who ate in your restaurant, who had you prepare their taxes, who had you adjust their back - whatever - has forgotten about you, your business and your product or service.

And unless you do something to nurture and protect that relationship, chances are good that you will never achieve maximum profitability from it!

I can already hear some of the grumblings: "My clients aren't like that" or "My business is different." I can't tell you how many times I've heard a client say: *"They know where we are, they know what we sell, when they need us again, they'll call."* To me this attitude is lazy, naïve... even arrogant. I'm sorry, but it is a load of crap and it's the exact attitude that keeps businesses (and their owners) small and struggling.

Please heed my warning: You can't assume that people will remember your business and come back to you when they need your service. Your clients are not automatically loyal. In fact, you should consider them indecisive, unpredictable and susceptible to the seductions of the marketplace. And unless you do something to continually jar their memory... to reinforce your relationship... to remind them of your existence... chances are good that you'll never see them again... especially in this economic environment!

As a strategic adviser and profit consultant whose job it is to find hidden or neglected profits in a business, I always look to an existing "herd" first to create immediate cash flow surges. And yet in so many businesses there are not only NO mechanisms or systems in place to collect names, but there isn't even a list!

So in this chapter we are going to discuss 3 basic steps for building a "fence" around your clients so that you can develop a profitable, long-term relationship.

## BUILDING A "FENCE" AROUND YOUR CLIENTS

Some of you might be saying: "Okay, Brian...you keep talking about fences. My clients aren't cows... they aren't on my property... I can't lock them in my store... how do I build a fence around my clients?" (Incidentally, the fence in my example is your RELATIONSHIP with your clients. In just a few minutes we are going to talk more in-depth about relationship.)

Let me introduce you to the 3 basic steps we are going to use in this book for building a fence around your herd of clients.

### STEP 1: COLLECT PROSPECT/CLIENT DATA

Your client base represents a gold mine. We've already discussed that it is more valuable than anything else in your business - more valuable than your offices, your warehouses - even more valuable than your top sales people.

What continually shocks me is that most businesses don't keep good records of their clients. I'm always amazed when a business does not capture every bit of information they possibly can about a client or prospect. Prime examples of this are MOST retail stores and almost every single restaurant I've ever stepped foot into.

What's almost worse is the company that does collect all of their clients' information and then once they're done with the transaction, that information gets put away somewhere never to be used again… ugh!

So depending on the quality of your list and your mechanisms for collecting names, we'll need to do two things immediately:

1) Begin collecting as much information as possible on each client that walks in your door or calls your business. (Ideally you want their name, address, email address and phone number.)

2) Go through your existing list and clean it up. What I mean by this is to put the list into an easy-to-use format (such as an Excel spreadsheet) and make sure that every record contains all of the information you need to be able to communicate with them. (Be warned: the older the information is, the less likely it is to still be correct.) Once you've compiled this list, there are services that can "clean" the list for you. (See the "Resources" section below.)

You might be thinking: "But Brian… I own a restaurant or retail store and people don't want to give me their information." Admittedly, it is a little harder to collect information in these types of businesses, but not impossible. The best way to get information from these types of businesses is to directly BRIBE the client. Here are a few simple ideas that will get you more names than you're getting right now:

- **Restaurant (under $15 average ticket):** Give them their first (or today's) meal free! If you don't have the stomach to do that yet, create a Lunch or Dinner "Club" and offer a special discount for "Lunch Club" members only. Make it super easy for them. Give them a punch card that can be redeemed for a free meal for every 5 (7 or 10) meals they purchase. Create a simple sign-up card that might look like this.

**Lunch Club Membership**
ENROLLMENT FORM

Name
Address
City State Zip
Phone Number Email address
Member Number

1234 Main Street
Anywhere, CA 92648
(714) 555-1212

**Papa's Place**

- **Restaurant (over $15 average ticket):** Offer a FREE appetizer, dessert or drink. Create a Dinner Club instead of a Lunch Club. The Dinner Club membership could entitle the member to anything from meal discounts, to special or preferred seating, to special Dinner Club events.

- **Retail:** Just ask at the point of sale. You'd be surprised how many people will just give it to you. Train your staff to automatically ask. Start with asking for their home zip code, then their full name. Ask if they'd like to be added to your "Preferred Client" list.

- Another idea that will work for either type of business is the proverbial fishbowl. Put out a fishbowl and hold a contest. Give away a free lunch every week...or even better...give away free lunch for a month. Or hold a contest to win something from your store - a suit, a sweater, earrings, a toy, a book, etc. Just have people drop their business cards into the fishbowl. You can even print up simple, basic cards on which they can provide their contact information.

But don't make the mistake that a lot of other businesses do with this strategy... at the end of every day, enter the information into a usable database. (Do this every day so the cards don't get lost.)

Keep something in mind... one way or another you paid to get that person to walk in your door or call you. Please don't make the mistake of letting them walk out the door without capturing their information, especially if they bought something! It's always going to be easier and cheaper to increase your revenues -- and profits-- by selling more and more to your existing client base.

## ORGANIZING YOUR DATABASE

If you don't store your client names in a usable database (anything from a basic 3x5 index card to a computer file), start doing so right away. The simplest and easiest way to do this is to enter the names into an Excel Spreadsheet. (See sample spreadsheet below.) At a minimum each client "record" should contain the following information:

NAME ADDRESS | CITY | STATE | ZIP | EMAIL | PHONE NUMBER

| NAME | ADDRESS | CITY | STATE | ZIP CODE | EMAIL |
|---|---|---|---|---|---|
| John Smith | 1234 Main St. | Long Beach | CA | 90803 | jsmith@yahoo.com |
| Mary Johnson | 1548 2nd St. | Seal Beach | CA | 90740 | mary@gmail.com |
| Brad Clooney | 780 Horton St. | Long Beach | CA | 90807 | brad@pitt.com |

Many businesses that use off-the-shelf (or even custom) CRM software should have access to the information (if it is being entered properly).

I work with a lot of service businesses and professional practices. These businesses almost always have client records, but many times they are filed away somewhere. If your business is "old school", all invoices are in triplicate and filed away in big filing cabinets, why not pay a high school student $8 to $10 an hour to go through all of your invoices from the last 3 years and create a database? They can do this using a simple Excel Spreadsheet.

**ADVANCED TACTIC:** While the student is in there looking through all of your invoices, it's easy to add columns to the spreadsheet and list each transaction type (what they bought), the value of the purchase and the date. For example... your spreadsheet may look something like this:

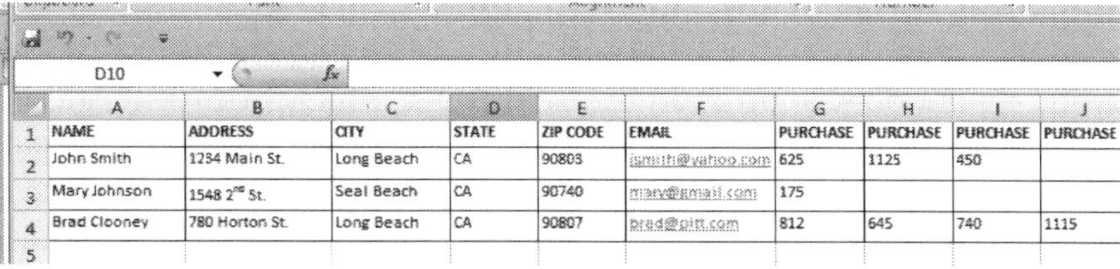

| NAME | ADDRESS | CITY | STATE | ZIP CODE | EMAIL | PURCHASE | PURCHASE | PURCHASE | PURCHASE |
|---|---|---|---|---|---|---|---|---|---|
| John Smith | 1234 Main St. | Long Beach | CA | 90803 | jsmith@yahoo.com | 625 | 1125 | 450 | |
| Mary Johnson | 1548 2nd St. | Seal Beach | CA | 90740 | mary@gmail.com | 175 | | | |
| Brad Clooney | 780 Horton St. | Long Beach | CA | 90807 | brad@pitt.com | 812 | 645 | 740 | 1115 |

Now I must caution you here; the point of this exercise is not just to collect names and do nothing with them. In the coming chapters we are going to discuss how you are going to use these names to flood your business with more sales. Here are just a few ways that your list has the potential of making you tons of money:

1. From this spreadsheet you can easily reach out to your current and past clients.
2. You can run simple mapping to see where your clients live.

This one piece of advice could be a huge advantage for your business. Imagine being able to look at a map of your business area and see (with the use of markers) where each of your clients live or work. I have done this for years. It helps determine where you should be marketing, where you should be spending your advertising dollars and where you shouldn't.

3. You can easily pick out your "best" clients and know what they are worth.
4. Once you identify your best clients, you can put together a strategy for going after more clients just like them.

Okay, now that we've got a system for capturing our clients' information, we need to begin the process of developing a solid relationship. How are we going to do that? Well we're going to start by acknowledging them for trusting us with their business and demonstrating our sincere appreciation.

## STEP 2: ACKNOWLEDGE & APPRECIATE

In this book I'm not even going to touch on the concepts of great products and service. I am going to assume that you are already delivering these to your clients, and are looking for ways to capitalize on your success. If you're not, I would suggest fixing some of those things before implementing the strategies in this book.

The whole idea of having a herd of clients who support your business is to make sure that they are getting the best of everything possible in your industry and that your business is known to be the one that goes above and beyond every other business of its type in your market.

When a client buys from you, he/she probably could have bought a similar product or service from any one of your competitors, but he/she picked you. This fact gives you a slight competitive advantage.

### What can you do to keep this advantage?

Everyone likes to be that "special" customer, client, patient, etc. Saying: "Thank You" is one way of letting your clients know they mean more than just another dollar to you - it's the first step in letting them know that they are appreciated and an important part of your business success.

So many businesses fail miserably in the simple act of thanking their clients for their business. Think about it... when was the last time you were sent a thank you note, or received a phone call from a place that you did business with... sad, isn't it?

Some business owners even go as far as having an arrogant attitude, acting as if the client needs them more than they need the client. In a few, very rare cases this may be true, but for most businesses this couldn't be more untrue.

Now I'm not suggesting that you keep unreasonable, unprofitable, unappreciative clients (of course the gratitude and appreciation must go both ways), but it is up to you to set the pace. I am the first one to suggest "firing" clients when they are unprofitable and use up a disproportionate share of your resources.

## SAYING "THANK YOU" THE RIGHT WAY

Over the years, I have developed a number of thank you and appreciation systems for our businesses and our clients (in fact, this is one of g|Four Marketing Group's specialties). Here I'll give you an example of 4-step approach we used for our (service) businesses to show our clients how much we appreciated their business. This 4-step approach will work for any business. Steps 1, 2 and 3 happen whether they are a new client or an existing/repeat client; step 4 is for new clients only. Here is what it looks like:

**STEP 1: (Within 24 hours)** Make a phone call (we call it a "happy call" and ask them: "Was the job/product/service done to your satisfaction? Was your service man professional?" And the most important question: "Would you refer your friends or family to our business?" (By the way, this last question could be the only question you need to ask. It is a powerful question.) You may even want to ask them: *"Is there anything we could have done better?"* I remember the first time I heard that question (from Enterprise Rent-A-Car), it blew me away. I actually stopped in my tracks and had to think about it... it's a great question.

**STEP 2: (Within 24 hours)** Send a handwritten "Thank You" note from the owner and/or the person who handled the transaction directly with the client. We buy simple preprinted "Thank You" cards with envelopes in bulk (you can get these at any office supply store).

After the transaction is completed and Step 1 has been done, the owner writes a quick note - in his/her handwriting. We give them a sample script (see below) but encourage them to personalize the card a little. Inside the card, the Service Manager will include 2 of their business cards, address the envelope (by hand) and then mail it. (It is crucial that this happens within 24 hours.)

**Here is a sample note:**

DEAR [CLIENT NAME],

THANK YOU SO MUCH FOR YOUR BUSINESS! I APPRECIATE YOUR CHOOSING [COMPANY NAME] AND I LOOK FORWARD TO SERVING YOU AGAIN IN THE NEAR FUTURE. IF YOU NEED ANYTHING, PLEASE DON'T HESITATE TO CALL ME AT (305) 555-1212; I'LL BE HAPPY TO HELP.

AGAIN, THANK YOU.

[YOUR NAME]

**STEP 3: (Maximum of 10 to 30 days after the transaction)** A letter from the owner, once again thanking the client for their recent business. This letter, however, should also include a special offer for their next purchase/visit (this could be a gift, dollars-off coupon, add-on service at no charge, etc.), and a referral request form.

The timeframe for waiting varies with the business. For some businesses this letter should be done within the first week or so; others could wait a month (I would never go longer than 30 days). The reason for waiting to send the letter is to give them a chance to require your services again, and the letter will act as a reminder of who you are and the products and services you provide.

**TIP:** To make this easy, prepare (or have your staff prepare) this letter immediately after each transaction is completed and POST-DATE the letter 10-30 days forward. Put the letters into an accordion-style expanding file (Office Depot Item #: 391181) labeled 1-31, and file each letter by the date it's scheduled to be mailed. Then check the folder each day for the letters that need to go that day.

Here are a couple of sample letters you could use.

YOUR LETTERHEAD

**THANK YOU!**

Dear [First Name],

Thank you for giving [company name] the opportunity to [service you provide]. We know that you have a choice when choosing a [your type] company, and we sincerely appreciate you choosing [company name].

Clients like you are what make our company successful, and we are committed to ensuring that every client's experience with [company name) is an enjoyable one.

If for any reason you weren't completely satisfied with our services - or have a suggestion or a compliment - please feel free to call me at [phone number].

If you were completely satisfied, please recommend us to a friend or family member who may benefit from our services.

Sincerely,

[Your Name]

YOUR LETTERHEAD

**THANK YOU!**

Dear [First Name],

I just wanted to say welcome! It's a pleasure to have you as a new [client/patient].

Because we are a very busy [practice/firm] and quite selective regarding who we accept as clients, you are now part of a very special, small group of [patients/clients].

Before your next [appointment, visit] I wanted to give you several free gifts that you should find helpful. I've included [several free reports we've published, back issues of our newsletter, reprints of articles we've written, discount coupons for return visits] and a few other surprises.

Thanks again for choosing us; I look forward to seeing you soon.

Sincerely,

[Your Name]

**STEP 4: (Immediately)** Client is added to the ongoing communication list. We'll be discussing this in greater detail in *Chapter 6*.

Depending on the type of business you are in, your average transaction size and your clients' lifetime value, you may also want to send a "Thank You" present - -something they'll want, keep and use.

By doing all of this for your client:

- You erase any potential "buyer's remorse" that may be in the mind of your client, his/her family or associates.

- You dramatically reduce — and perhaps eliminate — the refunds, exchanges or costly service expenses that come as a result of dissatisfaction or disappointment.
- You develop a closer relationship with your clients and satisfy their desire to be acknowledged.
- Your clients will know that they have a source for solving their problem.
- You give them reasons to feel good about their experience with YOU and your company.

And:

- You make the client more receptive to your next offer.
- You can solicit referrals and testimonials.

If you noticed, Step 1 in my system is a phone call. We not only do this to show our appreciation, but we are also using the opportunity to answer any remaining questions the client may have. Often they'll ask about things which lead you into selling an additional service, option or accessory.

I often hear from business owners who believe that their clients don't want to be "bothered" by communications from their company. This is definitely untrue; I have heard this excuse time and time again. The truth is... the owner is the one who doesn't want to be bothered. In all of the years that I've personally employed this strategy, we have had only a handful of people (out of thousands) tell us that we are bothering them. And you know what? We take them off the list. Chances are better than good that they were a lousy client anyway!

All of this leads us to the last step in the "fencing-in" process.

## STEP 3: COMMUNICATE (KEEP IN TOUCH)

A few years ago we had a bug problem at one of my offices. I don't remember if it was ants or something else. To take care of the problem, we went to the phone book and found a local pest control company. This company came out and did a good job. They did what we asked them to do - nothing more - and nothing less.

We were billed and we paid; the transaction was complete. We were satisfied and undoubtedly the owner of the pest control business was satisfied because he was paid without complaint and he got further validation that his Yellow Pages ads work.

What's wrong with this picture?

Here's what... **he let us go**. We were put back out into the world without so much as a follow up, a "Thank You" card, a leave-behind reminder of the company name... nothing!

Sure enough, a few months later we needed pest control again. What do you think we did? Do you think we went digging through our files to find the name of the first company again? NO! You know why? Because we were lazy! We didn't remember their name, let alone their phone number, so it was much easier to just go back to the Yellow Pages (or the internet) and start the process again.

I couldn't tell you if we used the same company again, but my guess is we didn't. Even if we had - and here is the sad part - the first pest control guy never even made an attempt to profit from us a second, third or fourth time. In my opinion, he doesn't deserve my business... he doesn't deserve to be wealthy... he hasn't earned it.

How many things could he have done differently? How many strategic things could he have done to ensure that we became part of his herd? Many...and we'll discuss quite a few in this book. But the fact of the matter is that he is too busy chasing the next job and working "in" the business on the unimportant busy work (remember Chapter 1?). He deserves to be complaining about how bad business is, how much he spends on Yellow Page advertising, how crummy his clients are, and that he's not making any money.

I know that's harsh, but you can't assume for a second that your clients are going to file your company's number away for the next time. You have to earn their business and their attention. If you get nothing else from this book, get that you can't assume that your "herd" is safe. Even if we had filed the company's number away, there is no guarantee that we would have remembered where to look. There is no guarantee that an ad from one (or more) of their competitors wouldn't show up at our door that day to lure us away. There is no guarantee that a friend or neighbor didn't refer us to their pest control guy, or that a salesmen from a competing company wouldn't show up that day.

This is how most small businesses leave thousands, tens of thousands, even hundreds of thousands of dollars in profit behind. Do you see why it's important - even CRITICAL - that you develop a relationship with your clients and put up that fence to protect and nurture your herd of clients?

In the next chapter I'm going to introduce you to one of the most powerful strategies in this book: increasing your client's frequency of purchase. There are many ways to do this and we will discuss quite a few; however, to really make it work and to get the most out of each client relationship, you must communicate with them on a regular basis.

Imagine if the pest control guy had taken the steps outlined in this chapter. Imagine how different his business would be just on this "minor" strategy. He could have successfully opened communication with us and made us a member of his herd. By making us feel appreciated, by making us feel like he cared about our problem (bugs), and by becoming our trusted (bug) adviser, he could have provided us much more service than he did. He could have taken that one-time $60 or $70 transaction and turned it into a relationship worth many thousands of dollars. But he chose not to...he chose to continue to struggle in his business. He has chosen to work in a business that will have very little value when it's time to go to market.

So what about you... what will you choose?

By completing the action steps in this chapter, you will have successfully laid the foundation for effective, profitable communication with your clients.

To quickly review... you are going to collect the names of every client who steps foot in your place of business and organize the names of every client you currently have in your files to compile a usable database of clients that you can begin communicating with immediately. Next, you are going to open the pathway of communication by developing a system for expressing your gratitude for their business.

Once this is done, it's time to begin the process of building each client's maximum value. By opening this channel of communication, you will have the opportunity to bring predictability to your business;

you will gain control over the traffic that comes into your store, your restaurant, your accounting firm, your carpet cleaning business, your computer repair business, your software company, etc. and you'll have the ability to create business and profits at will. Why? Because you will have a herd of clients who will look to you as their trusted adviser.

How great would it be if your business had some predictability to it? How fantastic would it be to look at your schedule (service business), your reservation book (restaurant) or your calendar (professional services) and know that for the next X weeks you are busy and that your business is maximizing its capacity?

This will take a little bit of work, **but once you do it your business and your life will never be the same again**. Not only will you enjoy more profits, but you will sleep more soundly knowing that when you wake up, your herd is safe and they'll be back to give your business more money.

# CHAPTER 6

## Double Your Profits STRATEGY #2: Increase The Number Of Times You Sell To Your Herd

In the previous chapter we discussed the importance of establishing a relationship with each of your clients. I introduced you to a 3-step system for fencing in your herd.

First, you've begun collecting the names of every client coming into your business. You have those names in a usable database and you have started the relationship on the right foot by showing them your appreciation for their business.

The last step is to communicate (which we will expand on here). As I've already told you, you are communicating with your clients for two main reasons: 1) You cannot assume that your clients are automatically going to be loyal. You cannot assume for a minute that the next time they need the product or service that you sell, they will come back to you. So you are communicating to protect your herd. 2) You are communicating to build each client's maximum value and to become their trusted adviser in your field.

In this chapter I'm going to introduce you to what I feel is the most exciting and powerful strategy for dramatically increasing your profits. That is expanding your business by selling more of your products and services to your existing client base (your herd)...more often.

In almost every business I have ever examined, I have uncovered a ton of neglected opportunity to sell to the existing client base many more times than is currently being done. Unfortunately most businesses are not set up to capitalize on this fact.

## LET'S TAKE A LOOK AT AN EXAMPLE OF HOW PROFOUNDLY POWERFUL THIS STRATEGY IS

I get my hair cut about every 6 weeks (even though I should get my hair cut every 3 or 4 weeks). Did you know that if my barber "worked" to get me in every 4 weeks the revenue to the barber from me would go up 67%??

If my barber has 200 regular clients and he was able to do this with only one-third of them, what would happen to his sales and profits? They would go through the roof!

Would it be hard to do this? **No**.

Would it be a lot of work? **No.** In fact, it's less work than the haircut!

Just think about it, how many times should a client purchase your products or services in a year? How many times could a client purchase your products or services in a year?

Stretch your thinking here. If you own a restaurant, the maximum number of times could conceivably be as high as 600 to 700 times per year! If you are a dry cleaner, it could be up to 50 times per year. A carpet cleaner could be 6 to 10 times per year.

Are you starting to feel a little sick thinking about how much money you could be leaving on the table? Are you feeling that in a minute you are going to find out how much? You are, but then we are going to devise a plan for capturing more of that profit!

You see, clients - left to their own devices - are not going to give us the maximum amount of business possible; it's just not going to happen.

Let's go back to the Cash Cow Ranch for a minute. Do you think our cows would come into the milking barn on their own every day? No way. We'd have to go out and bring them in. We'd record the day and the time they were in, how much milk they produced and then we would schedule their next milking...right?

In the same way, your clients are hardly ever going to come in as many times as they should, let alone could. Do you know why? The number one reason is because they are not asked.

So with a little bit of strategy on your part, you can increase the number of times your clients purchase from you with relative ease.

How?

Let me ask you another question. What if the salon, carpet cleaner or restaurant owner asked you -- at the completion of the transaction -- when you would be back? What if they gave you an incentive for coming back sooner, rather than later?

Here is a simple tactic that shouldn't cost you a penny to implement, but will undoubtedly have a huge impact on the number of times you get your clients to purchase, dramatically increase your profits.

## LOCK IN THE NEXT APPOINTMENT

One of the simplest tactics for getting your clients to purchase more often is simply by asking to set up their next appointment, their next buying trip or their next meal, at the completion of this sale.

There are literally dozens of businesses that can extract so much more money out of their clients and yet, they refuse to do the "work" it takes to make it happen. You know what's really funny about this? It's not all that much work.

An obvious example is the one I gave you above (the haircut or the manicure). But what about oil changes and tune-ups or transmission services...or the regular medical/dental checkup...or your annual eye exam? How about when it comes to getting your carpet cleaned...

preparing your will or estate plan...discussing your investments or having your insurance reviewed?

Do you tend to have these services performed later than you should?

Of course you do... we all do!

Now some of you are saying: "Sure that makes sense in that business, but my business is different." I'll beg to differ; let's go through a list of a few businesses here and see what we could do with them to lock in the next transaction.

| TYPE OF BUSINESS | TACTICS |
|---|---|
| RESTAURANT (DINNER) | 1. Personally invite your guests back two weeks later. You could hand them a "special" business card that had your name, phone number and a note that guaranteed them their table would be ready when they came in or that you would buy their appetizers, salad or dessert that night. Do you think they would give you their name and phone number so they could be locked in to their appointment? Do you think they would bring friends?<br>2. Pick your typical worst night of the week, say it's Tuesday. Host a "special event" on the 3rd or 4th Tuesday of the month. Use the same tactic above to invite people to that special event. When they accept your invitation (or show interest) capture their name and address so you can send them a reminder letter before the event. Capture their phone number so you could call them to "confirm" their reservation.<br>This one strategy could give you a huge payday every month on one of your "worst" nights of the week! |
| RESTAURANT (LUNCH) | Make up a small business card that contains an offer (Discount off purchase, 2 for 1, FREE side dish) and a spot for a date stamp. The card could say something like, "use this card on [date] and receive [offer]". I would buy a small date stamp from an office supply store and create a supply of cards with different dates stamped in RED. |
| ACCOUNTING TAX FIRM | B2B - Once you have completed the tax returns, schedule a quarterly financial review. Provide advice to your business owner client. Help him save money, act like his CFO. In fact, make the first meeting FREE and offer to continue providing the service for a monthly or quarterly fee. |

| | |
|---|---|
| RETAIL | There are countless tactics that could be employed here depending on the type of store you own.<br>1. If you own menswear or ladies' wear store, you should -- and could -- establish your business so that the majority of your clients shop by appointment only. This way they have your full, undivided attention and you have the opportunity to sell.<br><br>2. Depending on the type of store, you could schedule a seasonal "wardrobe consultation." So for example if the client has come in and it is summer, why not schedule a wardrobe consultation with them for the fall season, 3 months in advance? |
| FLORIST | You could also use a variation of the restaurant example above.<br><br>Ask your client about the next special occasion in their life. Ask if they'll need flowers for that occasion as well. Ask for the date they'll need the flowers and get their phone number. Call them a week before the date to confirm the order. |
| CARPET CLEANING, PEST CONTROL, MAID SERVICES, CAR WASH, WINDOW WASHING, HAIR/NAIL SALON | These businesses all lend themselves perfectly to this strategy and if you aren't using them, start doing so immediately. As the owner of this type of business, you know how often your clients should use your service (it's almost always more often than they think it is). Make sure that they are given the opportunity to use your services as often as they should. |
| DAY SPA, MASSAGE, MEDSPA | Before your clients leave, make sure that they know about all of the other services you offer. Always offer the next appointment. Education alone would probably get you the appointment, but use incentives (discounts, extra time, extra services) if you have to. |

Of course, not everyone is going to say "yes". In fact, most people will probably say "no", but what if you "closed" only one-third of the people and only half of them actually showed up? Do you think that could have a dramatic impact on your business? You bet it would, and the beauty of it is that you'll have done this without spending one extra cent in advertising or client acquisition!

So what about you? Are you going to let your client walk out the door without locking in the next appointment or visit? Do you want to come up with a way of securing the next appointment with your clients? Of course you could, but you've got to have a plan.

Here is an exercise to help you develop a plan for implementing this tactic in your business.

## EXERCISE 6a
## THE NEXT APPOINTMENT BRAINSTORM™

1) **First, let's figure out what your profit opportunity is from this simple tactic. You should have a few of these numbers from previous exercises:**

| | | |
|---|---|---|
| Your current average transaction value | A | $ |
| The average number of times a client buys from you now | B | Times |
| Subtotal – Current average annual client value **A X B = C** | C | $ |
| How many times could or should your typical client buy from you? Stretch your thinking. | D | Times |
| Subtotal – Possible annual client value **D x A = E** | E | $ |
| Your PROFIT OPPORTUNITY - the difference between what is and what could be. **E – C = F** | F | $ |

**2) How can you set up the next appointment or visit to your business? Quickly list the first 5 ideas that come to your mind:**

1. ______________________________ ☐
2. ______________________________ ☐
3. ______________________________ ☐
4. ______________________________ ☐
5. ______________________________ ☐

**3) Select your best 3 ideas - use the checkboxes - or rewrite your best ideas here.**

1. ______________________________

2. ______________________________

3. ______________________________

**4) What is required for you to implement your best ideas?**

A script for your staff.

An appointment/reservation book.

A staff training session.

Incentives.

______________________________

______________________________

______________________________

**5) What is your deadline for implementing this strategy?**

DAY ______________DATE _____/________/________

## COMMUNICATE THE 'RIGHT' WAY AT LEAST 12 TIMES PER YEAR

Once you have a client in your herd, we now know how important it is to communicate with them in order to develop the relationship.

Now there are many ways to develop a relationship with your clients. However, because this book is about making lots more money, I'm going to give you my #1 recommendation. Admittedly, this is not the fastest way but, it is the BEST way.

Your communications have to be interesting, engaging and entertaining . Your communication has to be educational. It has to be full of benefits. And it has to lead them to making the only rational decision they could possibly make -- to purchase more of your products and services, more often.

But it can't be any mindless communication like a silly flyer or sales brochures that talks about how great your company is, but says nothing about how your product or service benefits your clients' lives. It must be something they want to read and something they look forward to getting.

Without exception, I always immediately suggest to every one of my clients that they introduce a monthly newsletter. Whether you sell to consumers or businesses doesn't matter. A monthly newsletter can be a very easy and inexpensive way to stay in contact with your clients on a regular basis, not only adding value and profits to your business, but protecting your business from your competitors, and from their own apathy.

## THE UNBELIEVABLE POWER OF MONTHLY NEWSLETTERS

A monthly newsletter is one of the best ways to keep your relationship with your clients intact; it is one of the most powerful fence-builders available. Your newsletter will develop a persistent, personal relationship between you and your clients.

It keeps you and your company at the top of your clients' consciousness. It gives you a chance to sell some more products or to introduce new ones. It gives you a chance to continually educate your clients.

Recognize clients that have referred others to you; this will increase the number of referrals you get. If one client sees that others refer you, she may do the same.

A monthly newsletter is a must. It must be an essential part of your marketing mix if you want to keep your herd of clients.

Here are some of the reasons a monthly (not every other month, not quarterly, not via email, but every month, on paper, delivered through the mail) newsletter will transform your business:

- Your newsletter keeps your company's name in front of your clients. With each passing month you don't communicate with them, you risk them forgetting who you are. The newsletter minimizes that risk.
- It lets you more effectively catch clients when they have a need for your product or service.
- It helps you to create an invaluable referral program and constantly remind them to refer their friends and neighbors to your business.
- It makes your marketing budget more efficient by spending money to market to better-targeted people.
- It helps you move toward working with only the "best" clients.
- It gives you the opportunity to make seasonal, holiday related and other special offers.
- It lets you make "suggestive" selling.
- It lets you entertain and educate your client.
- And much more.

A good newsletter program is really designed to make your business less dependent on one-time, new transactions (which are the most expensive to make) and more about developing a relationship with those people who have already given you money.

But ultimately your newsletter is about nurturing and caring for your herd by protecting them from your competitors and proactively, strategically pursuing your target audience... NOT just sitting around waiting to see what happens next.

VERY IMPORTANT NOTE: Your newsletter should include you. There's nothing worse than a newsletter that is from a "company" with no human attached. People connect with people, not companies. Make sure your newsletter includes a personal message from you. Believe it or not, people will be interested in what's going on in your life and your family's life. The more personal you make your newsletter, the more successful it will be.

Some of you may be thinking that newsletters are expensive and you can't afford to send one out monthly. The truth is they can be expensive, especially if you use full color, glossy paper and have 8, 12 or 16 pages. But I am not suggesting that type of newsletter.

An average newsletter on an 11"x17" sheet of paper (folded in half so it has four panels), printed on colored paper with black ink will cost you between $1.00 and $1.50 per name to print and deliver.

In cases where budget is an issue, to keep the initial investment down I have suggested starting off with a simple 8.5"x11" sheet of paper, printed with black ink. This will reduce your cost per piece to as low as $0.70 each.

By the way, how I generally pay for a newsletter is to look at the business's current advertising and marketing budget. I look for poor performers, cut them out and replace them with the newsletter. I suggest you do the same.

I know what you're thinking: "I don't have time for a newsletter, Brian!"

I hear you! On one hand I'd say you should find the time because it is not only one of the most powerful tools for keeping and profiting from your herd, but it is one of the best uses of your time as a business owner. But the better answer is that you don't have to do this yourself! There are services available to make this process quick and painless. (I've included a couple resources on this books website.)

## BONUS: HOW TO USE YOUR CLIENT LIST TO CREATE AN IMMEDIATE CASH FLOW SURGE

In this chapter I've introduced you to 2 very powerful tactics that you can implement in your business today that will immediately push your business toward doubling (or substantially increasing) your profits.

I thought that in addition to these 2 tactics, I would include a bonus. Now this one will take a little work (and a little money), but it is the exact strategy that I use to bring about immediate cash flow surges in the companies I work with.

The strategy is very simple: go to your base of existing and past clients and ask them to buy from you again... today.

How long has it been since you wrote to all of your clients and asked them to buy something?

You see, if your answer is "more than six weeks ago," you are quite possibly losing thousands of dollars in revenue and profits.

## 3%

Here is something for you to consider; at any given moment, about 3% of our potential base of prospects and clients are considering - or open to - buying whatever product or service we sell.

If we take this statistic and apply it to the idea of the "herd", it means that for every 1,000 clients you have in your herd, there are 30 who are considering - or are open to - buying your product or service NOW.

What this suggests is that a carefully-crafted letter to your existing client base could lead to a significant number of sales. (Adding email and phone calls will significantly increase your results.) Let me be clear here, I'm not suggesting you'll get all 30, but you could get enough to make your mailing very, very profitable!

Surprisingly - in spite of this - many business owners find one excuse after another to put off contacting their clients: "It's too much effort to write a sales letter, get it printed, take it to the post office, pay the postage, and get it mailed." Or, "My clients will complain about getting mail." Or, "I don't know what to sell them." That's nuts.

The simplest way to may this work is to write to your clients and...

## MAKE 'EM AN OFFER THEY CAN'T REFUSE

Here are some ideas to get you started.

- Got a new product? Let your clients know while at the same time offering them a "Preferred Price" to thank them for their previous business.
- If you're a service business, how about: a "XX% Off Sale", or even better, a "$XX Off Sale" (dollars-off offers will generally out pull percentage-off offers); a "2-for-1 Special" or an "End-of-the-Month Sale"? The sale you have is limited only by your imagination.
- If you're in retail, consider doing a quarterly "Private Client Sale." This is a closed-door, invitation-only event, limited to

your regular clients. Hold this event once a quarter on a day when you'd normally be closed (or after hours), and make a party out of it. Make it fun by having refreshments, music, door prizes and in-store decorations. You'll be surprised at how much extra business this will generate every four months or so.

- If you're in the restaurant business, you can do a special "Family Spaghetti and Meatball Night."

**Want to "plus" this strategy?** Tell them they can bring a friend and then focus the event on converting the friends into paying clients.

Again, your offers are limited only by your imagination, and you've no doubt made them before in your general advertising. But in this case, make it only to your client base. Make it exclusive, just to show them how special they are.

**ACTION! Step**

Send a letter to your client list, explaining how you'd like to thank them for their past business by holding a special event or offering them a special deal. Make a powerful and compelling case as to the "reason why" you're offering them such a special deal. Give a reason why (or multiple reasons why) they should be interested in taking advantage of the product or service you're now offering and then lead them to action. Tell them exactly what to do and state the deadline.

You will be amazed at how quickly and how favorably they respond.

On the following page is an example of a letter that a restaurant owner (also easily adaptable to a retail business) might communicate - via mail - to their client base to get them to return for another visit.

## "I've Got a $15.00 Reward For Your Return"

Dear [first name],

It's been quite a while since we've had the pleasure of you [dining or shopping] with us. This is [your name], owner of [your restaurant or store's name], and I haven't seen you in a long time…quite frankly, we miss you.

So to shamelessly bribe you to return, I'm giving you a $15.00 [Number that fits your business] credit, good towards your next [meal/visit].

There are no strings attached and no obligation to return, but I think you will, once you experience our incredible selection of (specialty entrees, our award-winning chefs, our incredible wine list, mouth-watering desserts made from scratch/menswear/custom jewelry] awaiting you here at [name of business].

So please let us welcome you back to [name of business]. Here's all you need to do:

1. Give us a call at xxx-xxx-xxxx and make [reservation/appointment].

2. Let us know you've received this special "welcome back" offer so we can reserve one of the best tables for you and your party.

3. After the meal, when your check arrives, simply give this "welcome back" letter to your server and use it just like $15.00 cash.

I know you have lots of choices when you [dine out/ purchase anything], that's why I'm giving you $15.00 "on the house" for the opportunity show you how enjoyable your [dining/shopping] experience can be at [your business name].

But you've got to hurry. I can only keep this special offer open until [date - not more than 30 days away] because that's when the [tourist season] gets going and all my [tables/aisles] are completely [booked/full]. So, don't delay.

I look forward to seeing you soon.

Warmest wishes,

[Your name]

P.S. This letter is worth $15.00 to use any way you'd like at (name of business). Just bring it along with you and use it just like cash with no strings attached!

Don't you think some percentage of your clients would respond to that offer? Of course they would! Do you see how powerful your existing client list can be? All you have to do is intelligently work your list, and rework it over and over again. Your client list is a wonderful, often-ignored, under-utilized, completely-neglected asset, just waiting for you to profit from.

**PROFIT RESOURCE**

1) At www.DoubleYourProfitBook.com you'll find a number of resources for creating monthly newsletters. They range from purchasing newsletters already done for you, to templates that require very little customization that you can do on your own. And,

2) To help you make this strategy successful, and create a cash flow surge for your business, I have 4 killer sales letter templates similar to the one above as a bonus for you. You'll find one for each of the categories we are working with in this book: restaurant, service, professional and retail.

# CHAPTER 7

## Double Your Profits STRATEGY #3: Increase Your Average Transaction Value

In the last chapter we talked about the powerful strategy of increasing the number of times your client buys from you.

In this chapter we are going to talk about one of the most under-utilized of all marketing strategies... getting your clients to increase the size of their purchases.

At its simplest, this strategy suggests you offer <u>every</u> client a better or added deal, right at the point of sale. This could include offering a larger quantity at a bargain price, or "packaging" products or services in addition to the one the client is buying (complimentary products, special offers, etc.). The important thing to keep in mind is that 30% to 40% of the clients you offer this to will say "yes." This simple little technique could immediately and effortlessly "double" your profit and quadruple your cash flow.

This strategy is so easy and effective, that it's amazing so few people use it. Here are 3 reasons why this is so effective:

First, once the client has already decided to do business with you, he or she already trusts you (at least a little bit);

Second, when you get clients to make a purchase, they have to relax their grip on the purse strings;

Third (and most importantly), while the purse is open, it's generally really easy to get them to dig a little deeper.

It's advantageous for you because you've already spent the money to acquire the client, so any additional sales you make to them automatically carry a higher profit margin than the original sale.

In this book we are going to look at 2 specific ways to increase transaction value - the "bump" and the "up-sell."

## THE "BUMP"

Here is one of the best examples of a bump - it's easy...it's quick... it's painless and it has produced billions of dollars in add-on sales.

"Would you like fries with that?"

Most people immediately recognize this question. It is, of course, one of the most famous "bumps" there is and it started with McDonald's.

Try going in to a McDonald's® and simply ordering a hamburger and a drink and see what happens. The person taking your order will invariably ask you the "magic" question.

If you pay attention, just about every fast food place now does this in one way or another (and because of it, they are adding millions of dollars in sales and profits to their businesses). If they aren't offering you the fries, they are asking if you'd like the "combo" (chips and a drink), or if you'd like to supersize your order.

These are great examples of the bump, and I'll give you more in the next few pages. If you aren't bumping in your business, you are losing thousands of dollars of profit.

When putting together a bump for your business, it's important to think carefully about the product or service you are going to offer for a bump. Make sure that the product or service complements what they are purchasing. Otherwise, you may run the risk of your clients feeling offended.

## THE "UPSELL"

The main difference between the bump and the up-sell is that the bump is a suggestive sale that anyone can be trained to make. The up-sell generally requires a little more actual selling and therefore requires more thought and training.

In this case, you're going to sell some of your clients a bigger or better item instead of (or in addition to) adding a bump.

Simply show the client a version of your product or service that's better, bigger, or faster than the one he or she was considering, but with some special consideration such as a substantial discount, more favorable payment terms, extra options, or accessories.

Car dealers are masters at upwelling. After they've sold you the car, they will try to sell you all kinds of options, such as extended warranties, financing, etc. This normally adds $500 to $1,000 in additional profit to the dealer's bottom line. In many cases, this is where their only real profit comes from.

Always remember, a certain percentage of clients are going to easily move up and spend more money. That's added profit.

Now, let's get to work.

On the next page you'll find a table. Down the first column you'll see many different types of businesses (some of them you'll recognize); in the second column is an example of a bump for that type of business. The third column is an example of an up-sell. The last column is for you. Use the ideas from this variety of businesses to come up with ideas for bumps and up-sells for your business.

# EXERCISE 7a
# BUMP AND UP-SELL BRAINSTORM

| PRODUCT OR SERVICE | BUMP | UPSELL | YOUR BUSINESS |
|---|---|---|---|
| Electronics ( Best Buy®) | DVD's, accessories, batteries | The extended warranty | |
| Fast food Subway® | "Do you want to make it a combo?" | As I write this, they have just launched a new campaign – "Stop in for breakfast and get lunch to go." Brilliant. | |
| Furniture Dealer | ScotchGuard stain protection | Lighting, rugs, accessories | |
| Chiropractor | Package of treatments | Wellness products<br>Sleep products | |
| Carpet Cleaning | ScotchGuard stain protection | Ozone (clean air) machine<br>Marble polishing | |
| Florist | Extra greenery<br>Greeting cards | Balloons, candy<br>Buy your next occasions flowers today and save XX% | |
| Hair Salon | Hair care products | Skin care products<br>Manicure/ pedicure | |
| Clothing retailer | Alterations<br>Tie, shirt, socks and belt package | Additional suit at discount | |
| Landscape contractor | Better quality product (tile, stone, etc.) | Add garden furniture, TV's, outdoor accessories | |

Here are a few more great examples of how other businesses increase their average transaction value. Use these examples to expand your mind and extract ideas that you can apply to your own business.

You've undoubtedly been to a Costco; what's incredible about Costco is that they have filled their store with big, impulse-buy stuff. We're not talking a pack of gum next to the counter... we're talking big, flat screen TV's at (seemingly) ridiculously-low prices.

I don't know about you, but I always spend more time and money in that place than I ever intend to. In fact, I remember a few years ago when my girls were younger, they had these great sticker books for kids. They were about $7 and I bought one every time I visited Costco, for probably a year.

My favorite line about Costco is "I went in to buy a ______, spent $240, walked out and forgot to buy the ________." This is increasing the average purchase at its finest.

## PROMOTE "THE" ITEM

There is a restaurant chain called The Cheesecake Factory®... you're probably familiar with them. They have done a brilliant job of maximizing their client value. They have <u>conditioned</u> their clients to want -- no, to need -- a piece of their incredible cheesecake after their meal. What's brilliant is that regardless of how full you are from your meal, you just can't leave there without a slice of cheesecake. My guess is that the cheesecake adds significantly to their bottom line. If you've ever been there, it's an easy sale... the server just mentions cheesecake and you can't leave without ordering a piece!

If you own a restaurant, how can you recreate this?

Make dessert, appetizers or even wine a big deal. Prominently display these items in your restaurant, have your servers immediately mention that your guests have to order a dessert or appetizer and then offer specials on desserts and/or appetizers.

## ADD PROTECTION OR AN EXTENDED WARRANTY

Have you ever bought new furniture without the salesman asking you to add on the ScotchGuard stain protection? Probably not.

That's because when you buy a $1,000 sofa, it's not very hard to convince you to add stain protection for only $50 - $100.

I've heard that up to 80% buy the bump (the ScotchGuard protection), and it's almost pure profit to the store. Think about what this is worth to the furniture store. Say they sell on average 30 couches a week, 52 weeks per year. If they add $75 profit to each of these sales, it adds about $117,000 a year to the bottom line!

Any business can bump or up-sell. As long as the add-on is a legitimate value, with definite appeal and high-perceived value, and as long as the offer is alluring, you can apply the bump/up-sell technique to any business.

One thing is important, though: Be certain you develop a compelling, believable reason why you are offering the bump or up-sell so the offer has credibility.

How much can the bump or up-sell add to your bottom line? That depends on you. None of these strategies will magically work or on their own. You have to implement them and make them part of your everyday business. I will tell you that this strategy alone can double your profits immediately.

On the next page is an exercise to help you develop bumps and up-sells for your business. Do not skip this exercise. Nothing else in this book is as important to your business -- at this moment -- as this exercise is.

# EXERCISE 7b
# THE BUMP/UPSELL STRATEGY WORKSHEET

1. List 5 ways you could bump your sales, starting today. What are some simple, easy, natural add-ons to your product or service?

1a. ______________________________ ☐

1b. ______________________________ ☐

1c. ______________________________ ☐

1d. ______________________________ ☐

1e. ______________________________ ☐

**BIG! Idea:**

If you sell a product, make your bump or up-sell a service.
If you sell a service, make your bump or up-sell a product.

2. List 5 things you could immediately begin selling to each client at the point-of-sale. What could you offer that complements your product or service? What are natural add-ons to your product or service?

2a. ______________________________ ☐

2b. ______________________________ ☐

2c. ______________________________ ☐

2d. ______________________________ ☐

2e. ______________________________ ☐

**THINK: Packages, complementary products or services, extended guarantees, incentives to purchase in bulk, incentives to purchase products or services in advance.**

# EXERCISE 7b
# THE BUMP/UPSELL STRATEGY WORKSHEET

3. Select your best 3 ideas from both lists (1 bump, 2 up-sells) and rewrite your best ideas here.

1. ______________________________________________

2. ______________________________________________

3. ______________________________________________

HINT: You probably want just one bump. The bump should be as simple to execute as possible. More than one could get confusing. You can have a few up-sells depending on what is sold.

4. What is required for you to implement your best ideas?

A script for your staff.

In store/restaurant display.

A staff training session.

Incentives.

____________________________________

____________________________________

____________________________________

| WHO CAN HELP YOU IMPLEMENT THIS STRATEGY? |
|---|
| ____________________ |

5. What is your deadline for implementing the bump?

DAY ______________DATE _____/________/________

6. What is your deadline for implementing the up-sell?

DAY ______________DATE _____/________/_______

Remember, this tactic costs nothing and doesn't require any kind of hard sell. Simply suggest the appropriate option in addition to what the client has already decided to buy.

It's basically a numbers game. Even with just a mere suggestion of the bump, a certain percentage of people are going to buy it.

Regardless of what you do, the key to the whole strategy is to give your customers great service and a great deal. You're happy with a bigger sale and they're happy with a better deal. Under no circumstances should you use high-pressure, intimidating sales practices to force the client to buy more from you.

# CHAPTER 8

## Double Your Profits STRATEGY #4: Raise Your Prices

**Your prices are too low!** A very effective way to make more money in any business (without working harder) is to immediately raise your prices. You can do this with all your prices or just some of your prices.

Most business owners will strongly resist this idea and say things like: "My clients are price sensitive and won't let me raise my prices". "I'll lose all of my clients if I raise prices."

This is especially relevant in today's economy. In fact, many business owners think (falsely) that they have to lower their prices to get more business.

To this I respectfully say, "You are wrong."

Why are you wrong? Let's discuss just a few reasons.

Most people don't make their buying decisions based solely on price. Take a look at your own purchases over the last six months. How many products or services did you buy because they were the absolute cheapest ones available?

In most cases you will find that while price may have had an influence on what you bought, but it wasn't the only factor you considered.

Now, I will admit that there is a small percentage of consumers who are price sensitive. These are the ones who base their purchases solely on price. They are not buying from you because of location, convenience, hours of operation, service, knowledge, accessibility or any other reason... just price.

If you raise your prices, you will probably lose some of those customers.

These are the customers who typically take a lot of your time and interestingly enough, they usually don't spend very much money with you. If you think about it, they probably cost you more than they are ultimately worth.

My opinion is that if these customers leave, it may actually be a good thing.

I say that if - as a result of a price increase - these price-sensitive customers did leave you (and they probably will), it now gives you more time to devote to the clients who really appreciate what you do.

And the extra time spent with your more valuable clients will always produce increased revenues and profits... always!

Now some of you may be getting a little nervous here and may be tempted to skip this chapter; please don't.

I know the subject of this chapter will cause nervousness and queasiness in many of the people who read it and trauma in others. However, it is an extremely effective strategy and it would be silly for me to leave it out and for you to ignore it.

## WHY RAISE PRICES?

Almost every time I consult with a business, one of the very first things we do is raise prices or fees. Sometimes the adjustment is minor but more often it is pretty dramatic.

I do this for a couple of reasons: 1) I find that most business owners under-price their products and services; 2) it's my experience that price either isn't - or doesn't have to be - a very important factor in a consumer's decision or the success of a business. I raise prices because I know that I can justify why my client's product or service is worth the premium we are asking their clients to pay. You can charge anything you want as long as you can convince people you are worth it, and that's not very difficult to do.

For example, I have a private client I've worked with for the past couple of years. In 2010, I took his primary product that he was selling for $995 and turned it into 3 payments of $500, a 50% increase, almost entirely additional profit. (By the way, there was absolutely zero price resistance.)

Now I was happy with this increase (and so was he), BUT the problem was that we were actually doing his clients a disservice. It's a long story, but in 2011 I helped him re-engineer his business. We actually added more value to the service and raised his price from $1,500 to $9,000 (a 600% increase), then to $12,000. And interestingly enough, we've sold MORE at $12,000 than we did at $1,500. And mind you, we've done this in arguably the worst economy we've seen in decades! As simple and effective as this strategy is, the biggest problem is not the execution, but the emotional effect it has on the business owner. Fortunately my client (mentioned above) put his emotions aside, trusted me, trusted himself and followed the plan we created to build the additional value into his offerings.

In my work with entrepreneurs I find that there are a number of reasons why this is so difficult for a business owner to accept, but here are a couple of the biggies:

**FEAR**. I think the #1 reason is the fear that if they raise prices, they are suddenly going to lose ALL (or a significant number) of their clients. In reality this doesn't happen, but it doesn't make the fear any less real.

This fear is especially present post-2008. Many business owners actually believe they have to lower their prices to get business. This is ridiculous and NEVER leads to anywhere good.

To ease this fear, in just a few minutes I'll show you how you can actually lose a bunch of your clients and still increase your profits!

**OUR OWN LIMITING BELIEFS.** This is also a big one. Too many of us impose our self-limiting beliefs onto our clients. We make assumptions for them that are often untrue. We question what or how much they would be willing to pay for our products and services without a real understanding of what the client wants. But probably worst of all, we don't believe that our product or service is worth more.

The only advice I can give you is that this is a logical argument that you are making emotional. Take your emotions out of it.

## THE PRICING "STRATEGY" THAT ALWAYS FAILS

It's always interesting to hear the thinking behind why a business prices its goods and services the way they do. The amazing thing is that in almost every case, it's for all the wrong reasons! The most common pricing "strategy" is really no strategy at all.

Most of us do it the same way. In my early businesses, I came up with the pricing for my services by calling all of my competitors, determining what/how they charged and then figuring out if I was comfortable at the low, middle or high end of those numbers.

Now of course there are much more complex ways of coming up with pricing or fees, depending on the type of business you are in. Those are beyond the scope of this book, but I think you would agree that the method most business owners use is silly. It has no basis on anything other than the fact that it is what everyone else is charging. It does not factor in the value a client gets from their product or service.

You see, anyone will make a buying decision based only on price if they think all other aspects are equal or nearly equal. Do you know what this is called? It's called "commoditization".

Here's a perfect example of a commoditized business - the airline industry. How do you buy an airline ticket? You look for the cheapest fare to get you where you want to go. Why is it like this? Think about the experience. Once you're sitting in the airplane, do you even know if you are in a United, Delta or American jet? No. Do you care? No.

When the consumer believes that every dry cleaner, carpet cleaner, tax preparer, chiropractor, florist, computer repair or ____________ are the same, <u>they are left with no other basis to make a decision other than price</u>.

A consumer is looking for value. They want to know why you are different. They want to know how you can better serve them. They want to know what problems you are going to solve for them and how they will benefit by buying from you instead of the next guy. Your prospects are looking for value and confidence.

It's up to us to educate our prospect and convince them that we are different and that we provide greater value. Most businesses, however, do such a poor job of differentiating themselves from the next guy that the consumer is resigned. Why would anyone want to pay more for the same thing?

I want to keep this book as simple and straightforward as possible. So now that you understand how and why pricing is what it is, let me make a logical argument for increasing your prices using only facts.

I have always been at the high end of the market.

I like to be positioned at the high end of a price scale and have competitors focused on selling from the perspective of being cheaper instead of being better. In every one of my businesses, I have always been the highest (or close to the highest) priced provider.

I refuse to compete on price. Price is the laziest and riskiest advantage to market with. I would much rather figure out a better, different, unique way of packaging, delivering and selling my products and services and get the better non-shopper client at higher prices than to be the low price leader.

When I owned a bathtub-refinishing company, not only was I the most expensive guy in my market, I was one of the most expensive providers in the country! While every other refinisher was killing himself for $175 to $225 per tub, I was charging $495 to refinish a bathtub.

You know what happened? I sold more bathtubs at $495 than I ever did at $175. And when I went to sell that business, everything I did to become the highest-priced provider paid off big because I was able to sell the business for a substantial profit!

In my handyman business, over a five-year period we raised our prices at least 7 times. Do you know what happened with each price increase? Our close ratio barely changed - we sold just as many jobs - but we were getting a higher gross margin each time!

I could go on and on but the reason I've always been able to succeed at the highest end of the market is because I am confident not only in my products and services, but in the value that I provide.

You see, I'm always thinking in terms of value, never what the "typical" rates, prices or fees are that the rest of the market may be charging. I have also done a very good job of steering clear of selling any commodity types products or services.

So you might be thinking that you can't do that in your business. I'd say there is a way; you just have to think a little differently. Look at the bathtub-refinishing example. I was able to charge premium prices, and get them because:

I educated my prospective client about the process of bathtub refinishing (see Strategy #8 Educate for Dominance).

I offered them an unbeatable warranty. The standard industry warranty was 5 years; I offered a lifetime warranty (see Strategy #7 The Big Bold Guarantee)! As an aside, one of the problems with bathtub refinishing is that most companies used cheap products and wanted to get in and out of the house as quickly as possible. We experimented with different products, different application techniques, only bought the absolute best quality materials and added steps in our process, which gave our clients one of the toughest finishes available.

And finally - and quite possibly most importantly - when everyone else was focused on price or cost, I was focused on savings. Here's what I mean... at the time, the cost to replace a bathtub would be almost $3,000 and take about a week to complete.

My company offered our clients an alternative to replacement that would not require disruptive tear out, give them a bathtub that would be ready to use within 24 hours, looked just like new, would last forever and would save them 85% over the cost of replacement. Do you see the difference? Doesn't that sound like a better offer than: "Refinish a bathtub today for only $225?"

Now before some of you start thinking that this was somehow cheating because they could get the same service for half the price, you couldn't be more wrong.

My advertising promoted a benefit that most consumers did not know was available to them - refinishing vs. replacement. I was upfront with them in the educational component of the offer (see Strategy #8 Educate for Dominance), explaining all of their available options (that they could get a bathtub refinished for half price, etc.). So there were no sneaky, hard-sell or deceptive tactics used.

In Chapter 10, you are going to learn another powerful strategy called "Risk Reversal". This is another strategy that I frequently use because it works perfectly with increasing prices. We'll talk about it in detail later.

Okay, are you ready to have some fun? Let's get to work on hypothetically raising your prices.

Do you want to know what effect a price increase will have on your business before you do it? Do you want me to show you how you can lose a whole bunch of clients and make a lot MORE money?

## HOW IT'S POSSIBLE TO LOSE A BUNCH OF CLIENTS AND STILL MAKE A LOT MORE MONEY

Because the #1 fear business owners have when it comes to raising prices is the fear of losing clients, I developed a tool called The Price Optimizer Matrix™.

- The Price Optimizer Matrix shows us the immediate profit impact by raising prices.
- By entering a few numbers, it will show us how many clients (or transactions) we can lose and still make money.
- It will show us the effect on gross profit and at what point raising prices would be harmful to the business.
- It shows us how seemingly small changes could lead to huge increases in gross profit.
- It also tells us how much gross profit we can immediately add by raising our prices on a single product or service, a group of products and services or completely across the board.
- But ultimately, it helps us determine the right price increase.

Here is what it looks like:

**THE PRICE OPTIMIZER MATRIX™**

| CURRENT NUMBERS | |
|---|---|
| Time Period | MONTH |
| Current Sell Price | $ 150.00 |
| Number Sold Per | 500 |
| Item Cost | $ 75.00 |
| | |
| Gross Sales | $ 75,000.00 |
| COGS | $ 37,500.00 |
| Gross Profit | $ 37,500.00 |

**A**

| ENTER NEW PRICE HERE |
|---|
| $ 180.00 |

**B**

**C**

| % CLIENT LOSS | # OF UNITS | SALES | COST | GROSS PR | FERENCE | D QUARTER | D YEAR |
|---|---|---|---|---|---|---|---|
| 0% | 500 | $ 90,000 | $ 37,500 | $ 52,500 | $15,000.00 | $45,000.00 | $180,000.00 |
| -5% | 475 | $ 85,500 | $ 35,625 | $ 49,875 | $12,375.00 | $37,125.00 | $148,500.00 |
| -7% | 465 | $ 83,700 | $ 34,875 | $ 48,825 | $11,325.00 | $33,975.00 | $135,900.00 |
| -10% | 450 | $ 81,000 | $ 33,750 | $ 47,250 | $9,750.00 | $29,250.00 | $117,000.00 |
| -12% | 440 | $ 79,200 | $ 33,000 | $ 46,200 | $8,700.00 | $26,100.00 | $104,400.00 |
| -15% | 425 | $ 76,500 | $ 31,875 | $ 44,625 | $7,125.00 | $21,375.00 | $85,500.00 |
| -20% | 400 | $ 72,000 | $ 30,000 | $ 42,000 | $4,500.00 | $13,500.00 | $54,000.00 |
| -25% | 375 | $ 67,500 | $ 28,125 | $ 39,375 | $1,875.00 | $5,625.00 | $22,500.00 |
| -30% | 350 | $ 63,000 | $ 26,250 | $ 36,750 | ($750.00) | ($2,250.00) | ($9,000.00) |
| -35% | 325 | $ 58,500 | $ 24,375 | $ 34,125 | ($3,375.00) | ($10,125.00) | ($40,500.00) |
| -40% | 300 | $ 54,000 | $ 22,500 | $ 31,500 | ($6,000.00) | ($18,000.00) | ($72,000.00) |
| -50% | 250 | $ 45,000 | $ 18,750 | $ 26,250 | ($11,250.00) | ($33,750.00) | ($135,000.00) |

**A**

Here's how it works:

In order to use this powerful (yet simple) tool, you just need to input 3 numbers: 1) your current price or fee for a specific product or service. (You can also use an average transaction value if you prefer); 2) How many of these you sell per month; and 3) what it costs you when you deliver your product or service (so we can calculate gross profit).

**B**

Next, we enter our new test price or fee for this product or service.

This is where we get the data on the potential financial effect of the price change.

**C**

In the example above, here is what the matrix tells us:

The current sell price of the product or service is $150. This company sells 500 per month and their cost to deliver is $75. So they sell $75,000 per month and their gross profit is $37,500.

The new hypothetical price is $180. If you are a doom and gloom, fear-based thinker, here is what we know if we increase our price from $150 to $180. First, we can sell 25% (37) FEWER units and still increase our gross profit by 5% (from $37,500 to $39,375 per month) an additional gross profit of $22,500 over a year!

But that's not what excites me as that number represents just a small pay raise for the owner. What excites me is the opportunity for an annual increase of between $150,000 and $180,000!!

Now admittedly, increasing your prices by 20% or more and not losing very many clients is a little beyond the scope of this book, but it is not very hard to do with the right strategy and plan.

For our purposes here, below are a few examples using The Profit Optimizer Matrix that I've included because I want to help you get over the fear of not just raising prices but also losing clients. At the end of the chapter in the resources section, I'll give you access to this powerful tool and you can go and experiment with your own numbers.

Keep in mind that all the numbers are hypothetical and are for demonstration purposes only. When I work with businesses, I look at a number of different factors before suggesting any level of price increase. I am not making any personal suggestions; only you can decide what is right for you and your business. My commentary is for you to study and think about how it might apply to your business.

| **SERVICE - Carpet Cleaning Business** | |
|---|---|
| Current Average Transaction Size | $150.00 |
| Current Average Number Of Transactions Per Month | 250 |
| Current Cost Of Goods Sold<br>(Includes labor + burden, materials, plus equipment wear and tear) | $75.00 |
| Current Gross Profit Contribution | $18,750.00 |

Here is a quick table that illustrates what happens when you raise prices at 3 different levels. The percentage under the new price is the level of client loss:

| $165 | Annual Gross Profit Contribution |
|---|---|
| -5% | $ 31,500 |
| -15% | $ 4,500 |
| -20% | ($9,000) |

| $195 | Annual Gross Profit Contribution |
|---|---|
| -5% | $ 117,000 |
| -20% | $ 81,000 |
| -40% | ($2,250) |

| $225 | Annual Gross Profit Contribution |
|---|---|
| -5% | $ 202,500 |
| -25% | $ 112,500 |
| -50% | $ 0 |

So what can you learn from the above? Notice anything interesting? Using the $195 increase as an example, you could lose almost 40% of your current clients or transactions and still have about the same gross margin!! If you lose 20% of your business, you still walk away with over $80,000 in gross margin and having quite a bit of experience in this business, that would be almost all NET!!

Look at what happens when you go nuts and increase the price by 50% from $150 to $225. You could lose half of your business - YES half - and still make the same gross profit as you do now. But what's more exciting is to look at your opportunity. If this was done right, over the course of just 12 short months you could potentially add over $200,000 in gross profit, again which would be almost all NET! And believe me when I tell you that you would not lose very many clients!

| **RESTAURANT - High Volume Sandwich Shop** | |
|---|---|
| Current average transaction size | $7.00 |
| Current average number of transactions per month | 6,000 |
| Current cost of goods sold<br>(Food cost only) | $2.25 |
| Current gross profit contribution | $28,500.00 |

Here is a quick table that illustrates what happens when you raise price at 3 different levels. The percentage under the new price is the level of client loss:

| $7.50 | Annual Gross Profit Contribution |
|---|---|
| 0% | $36,000 |
| -7% | $ 9,540 |
| -12% | ($1,800) |

| $8.00 | Annual Gross Profit Contribution |
|---|---|
| -5% | $ 51,300 |
| -15% | $ 9,900 |
| -20% | ($10,800) |

| $8.75 | Annual Gross Profit Contribution |
|---|---|
| -5% | $ 102,600 |
| -15% | $ 55,800 |
| -25% | $ 9,000 |

The restaurant business is an interesting one when it comes to price increases. I think there can be a lot of price sensitivity depending on the level of the restaurant. For example, I think there is a lot more price sensitivity in a sandwich shop - like this example - than there is in a fine dining establishment. Price increases for fine dining or upscale restaurants are actually "no-brainers" and they really aren't very hard to do.

However, in this situation - a sandwich shop - it must be done with some caution. I don't ever want to raise price to the point that it has an adverse effect on a clients LVC or their frequency of purchase.

In this example, my advice would probably be to immediately raise the transaction value by $0.50, with the end goal actually being $1.00. The $0.50 would be such a minor change no one would feel it, and it's almost impossible that it will have a negative effect on the business. Next, depending on many factors including uniqueness of product, client loyalty and reputation in the marketplace, I would begin strategically planning the next increase. The immediate increase would put an additional $30,000+ in the owner's pocket; the next increase would nearly double his profits.

| **Small Software Company** | |
|---|---|
| Current average transaction size | $2500.00 |
| Current average number of transactions per month | 150 |
| Current cost of goods sold | $500.00 |
| Current gross profit contribution | $300,000.00 |

Here is a quick table that illustrates what happens when you raise prices at 3 different levels. The percentage under the new price is the level of client loss:

| **$2,750** | Annual Gross Profit Contribution | **$2,995** | Annual Gross Profit Contribution | **$3,450** | Annual Gross Profit Contribution |
|---|---|---|---|---|---|
| 0% | $450,000 | -5% | $ 666,450 | -5% | $1,144,500 |
| -7% | $ 166,500 | -15% | $ 217,350 | -15% | $ 913,500 |
| -12% | ($36,000) | -20% | ($ 7,200) | -25% | $ 117,000 |

In high transaction businesses, this really gets fun. Using the above example, if I'm selling software, I already have to make a case for how my software will make my clients' lives easier and more profitable. There is less price sensitivity when you are dealing with these factors. The other advantage that you have is that you can "finance" the purchase. By offering favorable payment terms, you can easily increase your price. For example, let's say that you sell a product like software or a service such as consulting. Your actual hard cost to deliver the product or service is relatively low. If I was selling the software in the example above, I would likely go for the $3,450 price right from the start and work my way up from there.

I would get the $3,450 by offering a 3-pay option (pay $1,150 for the next 3 months), or - depending on my actual hard costs - a 4-pay option. For those of you worried about "carrying" the balance (and believe me I hate receivables), I'm not worried at all about extending the payment time because I know I'm going to cover my hard costs on the first payment (which is very likely in these types of transactions). I would only perform this transaction with a credit card, so I can automatically charge the card on preset days over 3 or 4 months.

Also, because I've got an additional $950 to play with, I might add a bonus with a high-perceived value like additional support or a complimentary product or service that I know the business could use (like a 'How to Double Your ______ Business Profits' marketing system), or give them FREE tickets to the annual event for owners of the software.

I could go on and on, but I think you get my point.

As you can see, my job becomes fun when I am working to not only impulsively raise prices, but to implement a program that justifies and proves the value of the product or service at that price point. And in the process, a new "position" is created in the marketplace for the business.

In the three simple examples I presented above, there is a tremendous opportunity for increased profits (just like in your business). You can use this one strategy to give yourself an immediate 'pay raise' and do nothing more. Or, you can begin developing a strategic plan (using many of the concepts in this book) for implementing greater price increases, while minimizing the number of lost clients or transactions. Who knows... you may find that your new price point will actually attract more new clients because of the position you've created for yourself!

So before I turn you loose on The Price Optimizer Matrix, let me give you some final thoughts and pointers on this powerful strategy.

This not only makes the business dramatically more profitable, but also more valuable in the marketplace. So, who do you have to become in order to do this? What would your position need to be in the marketplace?

**Some Pointers:**

- The first thing to remember whenever a prospect objects to your price is that it's not about the money!
- When prospects tell you that your price is too high, they are really saying, "I don't see enough value in your product or service to justify the price." Or, "The benefits relative to the cost aren't clear."
- Earlier in this chapter we discussed the idea of differentiation and commoditization. The truth of it is: in the absence of any real differentiation, your client assumes all factors are equal and therefore is left to make a decision on what remains...the price.
- The reason the first question most people ask is, "How much does that cost?" is not because all they care about is price; the majority of the time it is because they have no idea what to ask and it is the only question they can think of that doesn't

risk making them look stupid!

Avoid discussing price until your client has had a chance to explain to you the benefits they want from your product or service. If a prospect wants to know the cost before you've asked them to define what they are looking for, redirect the conversation. Ask them what they want. Get them to describe the benefits they are looking for.

- Keep in mind the value that you offer your clients. Think in terms of the benefits (profit) they get from your product or service because ultimately, that is what they are buying.

  - A chiropractor doesn't sell an adjustment... he sells pain relief.

  - Mercedes doesn't sell a vehicle for getting from point A to point B... it sells comfort, style and prestige.

  - McDonald's® doesn't sell hamburgers... it sells consistency and speed.

  - An auto mechanic doesn't sell tires and oil... he sells safety and peace of mind.

**Spell out in detail the value of your products or services to your clients in everything you do.**

What can you do to start thinking this way? How can you program yourself to think in terms of delivering value? It doesn't matter what type of business you are in, there are at least a dozen ways that you can provide greater value than every other provider of the same product or service.

Finally, you must get past your FEAR of what might happen when you increase your prices. Remember your business exists to satisfy your needs. Dealing with clients who are only interested in price is a drain on your business and your life. I believe that eventually cheap prices lead to inferior work. Inferior work leads to unhappy clients. Unhappy clients leads to no repeat business and no referrals. So it's only a matter of time before the cheapest company goes out of business.

Remember, the real "magic" here is in what you and your company will become by implementing this strategy. When I made the decision to be the highest-priced bathtub refinisher, or handyman it forced me to do business in a new way. It caused me to ***be*** a different kind of company, a different (more serious) business owner.

When I re-engineered my client's business and raised his prices by a factor of 10 in one year, it forced him to get serious about developing a "real" business that provided tons of value to his clients. It forced him to become better at presenting his services to his prospects. It forced him to care more about his clients profit than his.

In the end, this is about value. The value you bring to your client; the greater the value, the greater your reward. Your customers and clients must profit (benefit) from your relationship. So, in many cases, by raising your prices not only do you enjoy additional profit but so does your client. Better service, better products, greater confidence, better experience... they deserve it and so do you!

**PROFIT RESOURCE**

Go to www.DoubleYourProfitBook.com right now. You will find a basic version of The Price Optimizer Matrix™ for your use. Use the matrix to play around with your numbers and see what happens – hypothetically - before making any changes. Once you've got an understanding of how a price increase will affect your gross profit (and ultimately your net profit), it's time to test a price increase.

WARNING!! Don't get greedy your first time out. Make an initial increase that you can be very comfortable with.

# SECTION THREE

## HOW TO EFFECTIVELY AND PROFITABLY ACQUIRE NEW CLIENTS

*"Ninety-nine percent of advertising doesn't sell much of anything."*

-David Ogilvy

# CHAPTER 9

## Double Your Profits STRATEGY #5: Use Only Direct-Response Advertising

Now that you've learned how to maximize the value of each client to your business, it's time to go out and get more clients. Now, every new client you bring in is immediately and automatically worth more to you than before you implemented the strategies in the previous section.

The goal of this chapter is to increase the effectiveness and "pulling" power of your current advertisements by 5, 10, even 20 times. Don't worry... this is not going to cost you a penny more than you are spending now.

While it could take a week to teach the fundamentals of a good ad, in this chapter I simply want to introduce you to the basic elements required to increase the effectiveness and "pulling" power of your advertisements.

I'll do this by introducing you to direct-response marketing. By the way - to help you better understand this concept - I'm going to bring in some help from advertising legend David Ogilvy. Ogilvy's books are must-reads for any serious student of marketing and advertising.

All advertising can be classified as one of two types: "image (institutional)" or "direct response". It is important to understand the difference.

Most advertising in magazines, newspapers, on radio, TV and billboards are institutional. They are institutional because in most cases they usually don't make an offer or ask for any type of response and as such, their results (or lack of) are nearly impossible to track and evaluate.

Here is an example of a typical image or institutional ad:

You've undoubtedly seen Absolut Vodka ads; they are in almost every lifestyle magazine available. This is one of their campaigns. You may not be able to tell from the image, but the man is pregnant. It's a clever ad... I guess.

To be fair, Absolut has spent millions (probably hundreds of millions) of dollars on these types of ads. Has it worked for them? I guess... they are one of the top brands in their category.

But let me ask you a few questions:

Is this supposed to be selling something today?

Does this ad make the ideal prospect put up their hand, get up off their sofa and want to buy something?

Can I gauge the effectiveness or profitability of this ad?

No. No and No.

So why run the ad?

According to Tim Murphy, their Senior Brand Director: "Our consumers are intelligent, and we hope they have a gut reaction that sparks conversations and challenges them to think about their vision of an "ABSOLUT World."

Okay Tim.

I guess if I was spending a large company's millions of ad dollars, and I didn't have to be accountable for the ads being profitable, I could get away with making statements like that and creating clever campaigns like this one.

This is a great example of image advertising. You'll notice in Tim's comment there is nothing about selling more vodka.

Can you or I afford to risk running an ad like this? No way!

But unfortunately I see local businesses doing it all the time.

The truth of it is an advertisement without an offer is just PR - public relations. And for a product like Absolut, they need PR and they need name recognition. But for most small businesses, we need response...we need the phone to ring...we need people to come into our business - TODAY - ready to spend money! For us, our ads need to sell something.

Most advertising agencies and your advertising sales reps like institutional advertising since - without tracking - they cannot be held responsible for zero results. If an ad campaign doesn't increase sales, they blame it on:

- The economy;
- The weather;
- Lack of frequency;
- YOU.

Advertising agencies are interested in being creative and cutesy. That's what wins advertising awards. I think this is ridiculous. Hey, I like cool looking advertising just as much as the next guy, especially if my name is on it. But the advertising field gives awards based on creativity, not results. Many ads that have won top awards didn't produce any substantial increase in sales.

My clients don't have millions of dollars to gamble. (Even if they did, I wouldn't recommend ads like these!) They don't have a big company behind them. They don't have years and years to wait for the ads to produce results. When they spend money on advertising, they need it to produce results... TODAY!

That's why I only use direct-response ads - because direct-response advertising is designed to get your potential client to take action.

Here are the components of a successful direct-response ad:

- ✓ Contains a headline that flags your prospect and gets ATTENTION;
- ✓ Creates INTEREST in your product or service;
- ✓ Creates a DESIRE in the prospect;
- ✓ Has a specific offer and an incentive to take ACTION... NOW;
- ✓ And, most importantly **we can measure the results.**

Why is this so important? Two reasons:

1. Most businesses have limited capital to spend on their marketing. Since you have a limited budget, why waste it on advertising that you can't measure?
2. Remember the sole purpose of advertising is - and always has been - to generate leads and produce sales. A direct-response ad concentrates solely on these objectives.

Before moving on I think it's important that I address an important topic here and that is the idea of "branding". Now, this is a very big topic and cannot be covered effectively here - and the truth of it is if we are talking about dramatically increasing the profits of a small business we don't need to discuss it - BUT, real quickly, let me give you my take on branding. For me and most of the clients I work with (start-ups to $50M companies) branding should be done AFTER the sale is made, not before.

In the case of Absolut Vodka branding is VERY important, they are all about "creating a brand", making you associate certain feelings with their vodka. So when you are out and in a situation that calls for you to make a choice... you'll choose their vodka. However, for you, for me and for my clients we are about generating leads today and converting those leads into money tomorrow. We don't have the time or budget to create a brand. Brands generally take many years and millions of dollars to develop (do some research on Absolut). You and me, we have to make money today. We can't afford to sink millions of dollars into our brand.

Now, there is definitely a place for branding in our businesses but it's not up front in our advertising. Unless you are a well known brand the prospect really doesn't care about your company name, logo or "pretty" ad. What they care about is what your product or service will do for THEM. However, branding does become very important (and affordable) once the sale has been made and after. When developing a long-term relationship with a client you want your name (your brand) to be "top of mind" with them. So all of your follow up communications contain your logo, your colors, your "look and feel" so they associate it all with YOU. So branding in our businesses becomes a by-product of making the sale and getting the customer.

## HOW TO CREATE A DIRECT-RESPONSE AD

A direct-response ad contains a headline that attracts the attention of the specific client you want. Then it makes a complete and compelling case for the reason for the offer. Next, it proves to the prospect that the reason for the offer will solve some problem in the client's life or provide some valuable benefit to him/her.

It provides specific reasons, facts, statistics and testimonials from other clients to validate the claims. Then it tells the client the reason why the company is able to make such an attractive offer. It tells the client what to do to gain the benefits of the offer.

It creates urgency by telling the client that he must act NOW in order to gain these important benefits, and why this offer is so limited, either by time, or by the available quantity of what is being offered.

Finally, it must contain a way for the business owner to track exactly what sales or clients were generated by that particular execution, whether letter, ad or postcard.

**Before going further, please read the last 4 paragraphs again.**

Because my intention for this book is to help you double your profits in six months or less, it would be foolish for me to attempt to teach you all about direct marketing here. Instead, what I am going to do is focus on one major direct response element so that you can quickly, and (nearly) effortlessly increase the effectiveness of your advertisements.

And that is by adding or changing the headline(s) you use to in your advertisements.

## WHY THE HEADLINE?

**Because 80 - 90% Of The Success Of Any Ad (or web page, blog post, email, etc.) Is The Direct Result Of How Well The Headline Grabs the Prospects Attention!!!**

Advertising legend David Ogilvy said, "On the average, five times as many people read the headline as read the body copy. When you have written your headline, you have spent eighty cents out of your dollar."

The only way your advertisement has a chance at getting someone to look at it - and act on it - is if it's noticed and read.

Too many business owners make the assumption that just because they placed an ad, wrote something in an email or website, blog post or Facebook everyone notices it... **they don't!** People are bombarded with thousands of advertisements every day; instead of assuming that they are seeing your ads, assume that their minds are busy with their lives and that they are half asleep any time they are near your ads. It is your job to interrupt and engage them. It is your job to get their **ATTENTION**!

## THE #1 MISTAKE BUSINESS OWNERS MAKE WITH THEIR ADVERTISEMENTS

The #1 mistake business owners make when creating their advertisements (online or offline) is using their name - or what they sell - as their "headline." Even worse is using their company logo!

One of the simplest, cheapest and fastest ways for you to increase the profitability of your business is to stop giving your name and logo the prime real estate in your ads.

Take a look at a couple of ads I pulled from my local yellow pages. These ads are right on top of each other and you'll notice that there is no compelling reason to call either one. In fact, they both break the first (and every other) rule of an effective advertisement!

To me, these ads are a complete waste of money.

If you want to get your prospective clients' attention and create money-making ads, you must appeal to their emotional "triggers" or "hot buttons." **It must answer the question: What's In It For Me?**

**Do either of these ads do that?**

There are two ways to emotially appeal to prospects:

(1) Convey how they can save, gain, profit, achieve or accomplish something through the use of your product or service.

This type of ad will appeal to your prospects' mental, physical, financial, social, economic or emotional well-being.

(2) Show them how - through the use of your product or service - they will avoid or minimize risks, worries, losses, mistakes or embarrassment.

This type of ad quickly suggests ways to decrease fears of economic ruin, discomfort, boredom, sickness, loneliness or prestige.

## SO HOW DO YOU WRITE SUCH HEADLINES?

First, remember that you're writing to an individual. A human being. Wife, mother, sister, brother, father, husband. Think of your ideal prospect - his or her needs, wants and desires - as they pertain to your product or service. Always write to that one person, not to a group or general audience. (In one of my businesses all of the advertising & sales materials I create is designed with one of my best clients, Charlie, in mind.)

Always personalize your product or service and your company. Never write in terms of "we" or "us." Write from the viewpoint of "you" and "yours." Don't write about how great you think your company is and how you have the best products or prices in town. Write how your product/ service will benefit him/her, what he/she will experience when he/she starts using your product or service. Make him/her feel that your ad is directed at him/her. Appeal to your propects' emotions.

> *"A headline should appeal to the reader's self-interest. It should promise the reader a benefit."*
>
> **-David Ogilvy**

**Keep in mind that on average, you have between 1.5 and 4 seconds to get your prospect's attention**. So you've got to grab their attention quick. As you write, imagine that your typical client is standing immediately in front of you. What would you say to him to grab his attention in a couple of seconds? Remember that your reader doesn't care about your need to make a profit or about what nice people you have at your company. He/she cares only about what you can do for him/her in solving some particular need or problem. Your headline (and body copy and offer) must convey benefit(s) to him/her...

## THE SIMPLE TRICK TO WRITING "KILLER" HEADLINES

Allow me to take you "behind the curtain" - if you will - and show you how I was taught to come up with headlines.

First, successful headlines are passed down from one writer to the next. What I mean by this is that copywriters don't reinvent the wheel every time they attempt to write a headline. No, they go to their "swipe files" of successful ads and sales letters to look for ideas, find a headline formula that works for whatever they are selling and then adapt them for their use.

As my friend Bill Quinn (author, copywriter and internet-marketing genius) says: *"Why create mediocrity when you can copy genius?"*

So let's say that I need to write an ad for your business. What I would do is go to my headline "bank". I would go through hundreds of proven headlines (some over 100 years old) and get a list of ones that I think might be effective. Below are some headlines that I pulled from a list of The 100 Greatest Headlines Ever Written:

Dare to be Rich

Do You Make These Mistakes In English?

Five Familiar Skin Troubles - Which Do You Want To Overcome?

Who Else Wants Lighter Cake - In Half The Mixing Time?

Need More Money?

How To Give Your Children Extra Iron - These 3 Delicious Ways

Guaranteed To Go Through Ice, Mud or Snow - Or We Pay The Tow!

The Truth About Getting Rich

The Secret To Being Wealthy

A Startling Fact About Money

7 Ways To Collect Your Unpaid Bills

A Little Mistake That Cost A Farmer $3,000 A Year

Advice To Wives Whose Husbands Don't Save Money - By A Wife

How I Improved My Memory In One Evening

How I Made A Fortune With A "Fool Idea"

How A "Fool Stunt" Made Me A Star Salesman

Now let's write a few headlines. We'll start with one for selling tax preparation services. Here's what we could do - take the headline: "The Truth About Getting Rich" and rewrite it to:

**"The Truth About Getting Your Tax Refund Fast"**

If I wanted to improve it, we could combine it with "7 Ways To Collect Your Unpaid Bills" and get the new headline:

**"The Truth About Getting Your Tax Refund Fast.**
**7 Common Mistakes Tax Preparers Make."**

Or we could use: "Five Familiar Skin Troubles - Which Do You Want To Overcome?" and rewrite it to:

**"Five Familiar Tax Problems -**
**Which Do You Want To Overcome?"**

Now remember this is meant to grab someone's attention while they're reading a newspaper, magazine, web site, etc. and get them to look at your ad. Once you get them to look you have to give them a good reason why they should call you right now.

Here's another example for a bathroom remodeling business. We could take the headline: "Who Else Wants Lighter Cake - In Half The Mixing Time?" and rewrite it to:

**"Who Else Wants a Complete Bathroom Remodel**
**– In Half The Time?"**

For a chiropractor, we could take the headlines: "The Secret To Being Wealthy" and "A Startling Fact About Money" and rewrite them to:

**"The Secret To Being Pain Free"**

*Or*

**"A Startling Fact About Back Pain"**

What about the mattress retailer ads I showed you earlier? We could take: "How To Give Your Children Extra Iron - These 3 Delicious Ways" and rewrite it to:

**"How To Get a Good Night's Sleep - 3 Simple Ways"**

As you can see, these headlines are probably much more effective at getting your prospective clients' attention, than putting the name of the business or what you do at the top of the ad.

## SUPERCHARGING YOUR HEADLINES

You could supercharge the effectiveness of almost any headline by adding a few extra words; here they are:

"Quick and easy", "Guaranteed" or "Free"

In the example above - to give the headline a little extra pulling power - I might take out the "3 Simple Ways" and replace it with the word "Guaranteed!"

**"How To Get a Good Night's Sleep... GUARANTEED!"**

*Or*

**"The Quick And Easy Way To A Good Nights Sleep!"**

Writing headlines is not easy. I have given you a formula that simplifies the process, but writing headlines takes practice and much trial and error. I have read and studied countless books, thousands of pages of information and written and used hundreds of headlines, and I'm still learning. Don't just quickly adapt any headline and run with it. Take your time with the process. Write out a dozen headlines before deciding on the one that you will test.

Once you've got your headline, make sure it is the most prominent visual on your ad.

Finally, be sure your headline answers the big question on your prospects mind:

***"WHAT'S IN IT FOR ME?"***

If they don't immediately get a compelling answer to this question, they simply won't respond to your advertising.

**PROFIT RESOURCE**

Go to www.DoubleYourProfitBook.com and download the workbook, 12 Fill-In-The-Blank Headline Templates. This workbook is a super shortcut and will help you craft "killer" headlines using 12 proven headline templates.

# CHAPTER 10

## Double Your Profits STRATEGY #6: Use Big, Bold Guarantees

ace the facts. The marketplace is cautious and lazy about buying anything (especially in the "New Economy"). And we all lose a ton of business because of the hesitancy of our prospects to take action!

Think about yourself... what have you purchased (or thought about purchasing) in the last few months? Maybe it was a car, a kitchen remodel, accounting services, carpet cleaning, software, video games, wine, food or dry cleaning.

Was it a confident, quick purchase or did it take some time? Did you do your research, surf the internet, visit different stores and/or make phone calls? Did you think about it for awhile and then finally convince yourself to just do it? Or did you talk yourself out of it?

Once you did make up your mind, did you take immediate action or did the purchase get put off because you got distracted or something came up that was more important?

### COMBATING THE HESITANCY OF YOUR PROSPECTS TO TAKE ACTION

What holds people back from making a buying decision and taking action right now? In almost every case, it's fear. People are practically paralyzed by the fear of making wrong decisions.

And wrong decisions can be based on any number of factors. They may feel that they didn't buy from the right place, they may question whether or not they really need the product or service or they may feel that they are paying too much.

Would you agree with me that if you can overcome that fear or reluctance to take action that you'll get a lot more business?

If your answer is "yes", then here is one of the most powerful strategies for helping potential clients overcome their fear or reluctance to do business with you... the use of BIG, BOLD GUARANTEES.

## THE USE OF BIG, BOLD GUARANTEES

People want to do business in an establishment where they'll be taken care of, not taken advantage of. A recent survey asked the question: "Why do you buy where you buy?" And no, the number one answer was NOT price (actually "price" was number five). The number one reason people buy where they do is CONFIDENCE. Confidence in the company... in the people... in the service.

How do you build a prospect's confidence? How do you ease their fears about buying the product or service you sell and of doing business with you in general?

What if you guaranteed that you would make the process easier, faster, cheaper, less-risky and with less hassle? What if your guarantee included the added benefit that if you didn't make the process faster, cheaper, less-risky and with less hassle, they would get their money back, quickly and easily?

Here's your opportunity to stand apart from your competitors in the eyes of your prospects. It's your chance to address an issue or concern they may have and reverse their general lack of trust as a consumer.

Is this bold? YES.

Is it risky? From my experience, NOT AT ALL.

Possibly one of the greatest consumer success stories of the last half of the $20^{th}$ century was built on the foundation of the following guarantee:

***"... fresh, hot pizza delivered to your door in thirty minutes or less, guaranteed."***

Not only did that guarantee create one of the most successful pizza chains of all time, but it set a new standard by which all other pizza-delivery companies would be measured.

Practical experience continues to prove that: (1) a guarantee boosts sales; and (2) the better the guarantee, the better the sales. The numbers will always work in your favor if you offer a guarantee.

By the way, if you refuse to execute this strategy... to even entertain the idea and test it...that throws up a big warning flag to me. First, I probably wouldn't work with you if you were a private client. This strategy is way too powerful to be afraid to use. But the other thing that would concern me is that your business is somehow unethical. You see, it is my belief that if you cannot, will not, or are too afraid to guarantee your product or service to the degree I am suggesting here, you need to find something else to sell.

## OK BRIAN, YOU'VE GOT ME TAKING MY CLIENTS' FEARS AWAY, BUT WHAT ABOUT MINE?

The first thing I hear when I recommend this strategy is the 27 different ways that prospects and clients are going to rip off the business owner. With the exception of Strategy #4 (Raise Your Prices), this is the strategy that generates the most "emotional interference." And usually, the emotional interference is strongest when the topic of "money" is discussed.

So this section is designed to allay your fears and help you think through this strategy - logically - in order to discover the enormous profitable benefits that it contains. However, if you are excited about this strategy and want to move onto creating your guarantees, skip this section and move on to take action.

Your first reaction might be: "I can't afford to do that; I'll have people calling me all the time wanting this or that - or worse yet - they'll want their money back and rip ME off!"

I have noticed that many small-business owners are constantly afraid of being taken advantage of. You're not alone. Believe me, when I first learned this strategy, I was concerned too. But once I discovered the "secret" behind it and the power it possesses, I continued to use it in every one of my businesses with great success.

Want to know the secret? From my experience - almost without exception - the amount of additional business you'll enjoy as a result of this strategy will more than offset the cost of those (very) few people who will take advantage of you.

Here is the truth: More than likely, if a client comes back to you with a problem, complaint or a change of mind, you'd probably do whatever you could to make it right, even if it meant giving him back his money...right? I hope so. Doesn't this mean that one way or another you already have some sort of guarantee, even if it's not promoted or advertised? So why not make it an explicit benefit of doing business with you?

What I'm suggesting is to take what is "unsaid" and start promoting it as a benefit of doing business with you! This will give you a huge competitive advantage over every other provider of your product or service.

Guarantees come in many forms, but for our purposes we are going to discuss just three: 1) the time guarantee; 2) what I call the 'negative-trait' guarantee; and 3) the risk-transfer guarantee.

To be clear, you don't have to employ all 3 types, but like everything else presented throughout this book, the more you "stack" and employ simultaneously, the faster and greater your results will be.

## TIME GUARANTEE

This one is simple and really doesn't require any work. It goes like this: if the typical guarantee for your industry is 90 days, make yours one year; if it's 1 year, make yours 3, 5, or even more.

Let me give you an example from one of my businesses. The typical guarantee period in the industry was 5 years. I advertised, promoted and offered my clients a LIFETIME warranty. This actually accomplished a few things for me.

It gave me a significant competitive advantage because I offered a guarantee that was longer than what anyone else was offering (or would offer). It also gave my clients confidence that they were going to get a better job than anything else available.

It allowed me to dramatically increase my prices, leading to significantly higher PROFITS.

I'll let you in on a little secret. I didn't just throw the lifetime warranty out there to see if it would work; I did a little research and I noticed something interesting. If the job was going to fail and we were going to get a call back, it was almost always within the first 90 days after we completed the job. So it really didn't matter if our warranty was 1 year, 5 years, 10 years or a lifetime. I'd be willing to bet that there is a similar actuality in your business.

## THE 'NEGATIVE-TRAIT' GUARANTEE

This is one of my favorites. Every industry has some negative trait(s) associated to it. They are generally found in the pain associated with working with that particular service.

For example, what is a negative trait generally associated with a plumber, carpet cleaner, window washer, handyman, or other home service contractor? A biggie for that industry is that the serviceman will show up on time (if he shows up at all). So what if your guarantee was that your serviceman would definitely show up and be on time?

If you wanted to increase the effectiveness or power of your guarantee, you may guarantee several negative traits at once!

One of the best negative-trait guarantees I've written was for my handyman business. The guarantee - which doubles as a headline in ads (see Strategy #5) - goes like this:

**"Your Handyman Will Show Up On-Time,<br>Be Professional And Do Your Job Right...<br>Or The Work Is FREE!"**

I know that many people don't have half an hour to wait to be served lunch, especially in these times. So let's say a restaurant does a lot of lunch business (or wants to do more); a great guarantee for them could have to do with wait times. "You'll be served your meal within 7 minutes of ordering, or you don't pay." Another issue could be that people are uncertain about your food, so you may guarantee they'll enjoy their meal. For example: "Try anything on the menu... try something new... go ahead, be brave. If for any reason you don't like it, we'll replace it with another item of your choice, within XX minutes!"

Okay, so those are great "minor" guarantees, but here is one of the most powerful guarantees you can offer. This guarantee is so good, it has the potential of dramatically increasing your conversion (from prospect to buyer) rates. Ready?

## THE RISK-REVERSAL GUARANTEE

Most business owners never realize that whenever a sales proposition is offered to a prospective client, someone has to take the risk - either the seller or the buyer. In most cases - especially in small business - the company makes the buyer assume the risk in the transaction. That's a big mistake.

The risk-reversal guarantee is transferring the risk of purchase from the buyer, prospect or client to the seller. I always use it. Taking the risk off the prospect and placing it solely on you indicates how confident you must surely be in the performance, quality and level of client satisfaction of your product or service.

When I think of how many people are "sitting on the fence" (not quite sure whether to buy or not) your risk-free guarantee may just give them the confidence to let you serve them and make them a satisfied client, instead of just passing by.

By turning the tables and taking all the risk off the buyer (and assuming it yourself) you make your sales proposition so much more powerful and appealing that considerably more clients and prospects will take advantage of your offer.

Before you get scared about reversing the risk onto yourself, let me tell you this irrefutable fact. When a company reverses the risk and assumes the risk for the prospect or client, the opportunity for double- or triple-digit sales increases are often the result.

Think about what would happen if you were able to double your conversion rates. Yes, a few clients will take advantage of your guarantee. When it happens - and it will - just chalk it up to a cost of doing business just like your rent, electric bill, or any other part of your overhead. Remember that as a rule, so many more people will buy your product/service from this strategy that the refund or return levels are virtually unimportant.

Imagine the impact you'll have on your prospects when you teach them all about your product or service and show them all of the benefits and advantages that they'll realize. They're just about ready to say "YES"... they realize what a great value your offer really is... now you've got them seriously thinking about whipping out the credit card.

Then you tell them or show them your guarantee which says:

> 100% RISK-FREE GUARANTEE!
> If, after you purchase ______________ [product or service], you feel for any reason that it fails to live up to our promises (or even if it does and you just change your mind), simply bring it back to us and we'll immediately and cheerfully give you a 100% refund of the purchase price. No questions asked!

**You'd have to agree, an offer like this is almost impossible for a qualified prospect to ignore.**

When you understand and use the concept of risk-reversal to your advantage, you'll become virtually unstoppable in your market area. And as long as your product or service is an honest value, the only outcome will be profits almost beyond belief.

Finally, here are a few tips when using the guarantee strategy:

- Make your offer as powerful as possible. A 60-day guarantee is good, but a 1-year guarantee is better.
- Once you've developed your guarantee, use it in all of your marketing and advertising materials, including your business cards. Make it a point to repeat or refer to it often throughout all of your advertising and sales presentations. If you own a store, post it on your walls. If you own a restaurant, put it on your menu. If you own a service company, put it on your proposals or estimates.
- Make sure your staff understands the guarantee and uses it to sell more of your product or service. Make sure they know that you are SERIOUS about the guarantee.

- If your guarantee or warranty is stronger than your competitors', make sure that you call attention to this fact.
- Most importantly, when someone does return your product or is unhappy with your service, DO NOT make it difficult for them to get a refund. In fact, make it as easy as possible. Give them their refund immediately. Do it with a smile. DO NOT make them feel like an idiot. DO NOT embarrass them. Word will spread both positively and negatively about how you handle your guarantees and how genuine you are about your offer. Don't take the chance of killing the effectiveness of this strategy over the few dollars you might lose on a refund or even a few refunds.
- Don't be afraid. This strategy is too powerful and too effective to be afraid of. You must think in terms of the additional sales you will enjoy, not the refunds you will give.

On the following pages you'll find an exercise to help you come up with your own big, bold guarantee.

# EXERCISE 10a
# THE BIG, BOLD GUARANTEE WORKSHEET

### 1. The Time Guarantee

a) What is your current time guarantee for your product or service?

________________________________________

b) What is the industry average or norm?

________________________________________

c) How can you significantly increase the number?

________________________________________

d) Will it make a difference in the number of products or services you will sell? If no, move on to the next guarantee; if yes, list what needs to happen (if anything) for you to increase or promote the guarantee.

1. ____________________________________ ☐
2. ____________________________________ ☐
3. ____________________________________ ☐

### 2. The Negative-Trait Guarantee

What are the negative traits associated with your business or industry? Brainstorm 5 ways you could use those negative traits in a powerful guarantee.

1. ____________________________________ ☐
2. ____________________________________ ☐
3. ____________________________________ ☐
4. ____________________________________ ☐
5. ____________________________________ ☐

### 3. Risk-Reversal Guarantee

What causes your prospects' hesitancy in purchasing your product or service? What fears, concerns or challenges do you have to address to eliminate that hesitancy?

List 5 ways you could eliminate the hesitancy by transferring the risk of purchasing your product or service from your client to you (where it belongs).

1. ______________________________ ☐

2. ______________________________ ☐

3. ______________________________ ☐

4. ______________________________ ☐

5. ______________________________ ☐

THINK: Try our product for XX days and if you don't see the benefit it offers, return it for a full refund. Even better, we'll come pick it up and refund all your money. We'll do [your service] a [certain way] or you don't pay. If we don't do [service] right within XX [time frame], your service is free.

**Select your best 3 ideas from all three types of guarantees and create your new big, bold guarantee.**

1. ______________________________

2. ______________________________

3. ______________________________

# CHAPTER 11

## Double Your Profits STRATEGY #7: Use Testimonials

Here is the strategy in a nutshell.

Go to your current clients and ask them to tell you about their experience with your business. Take a video camera with you (your iPhone is good enough), then take what they've said and use it in all of your advertisements and sales presentations. Print them up and put them in your store, include them on your menus and brochures, and post them on your website.

The reason this strategy is so effective is simply because...

**...what others say about you is 1,000 times more believable (and powerful) than what you say about yourself and your business.**

One of the most common ways that businesses get new clients is through word-of-mouth. Think about it. Would you be more likely to try a new restaurant if your neighbor told you how wonderful it is or if you saw an ad in the newspaper for it?

Of course you'd be more likely to try it if your neighbor couldn't stop raving about it. However, the problem with word-of-mouth is that you never really know when it's happening, so you don't have any control over the process.

But by collecting what your clients have to say about your business, you will have the ability to use those comments at any time and in any place that a new prospect may be looking for your product or service. This has the potential of giving you "controlled" and consistent word-of-mouth marketing.

## WHAT MAKES A GOOD TESTIMONIAL?

Good testimonials are specific; they say things like:

*"I increased my profits by $54,600 from just two of your strategies."*

*"From the minute we walked in, we were treated like movie stars! We were greeted by your hostess, Heather, and escorted to our table. Within minutes Mario showed up with a complimentary appetizer from your chef. He told us about the specials and suggested a wonderful bottle of wine. From the first course through the last, the food and service was amazing; thank you for an unforgettable experience!"*

*"Tech support spoke to me in plain English and indentified my problem in 90 seconds."*

Vague testimonials don't really tell the prospect anything. A vague testimonial reads like:

*"Your course was great. Thanks!"*

*"I got great results."*

*"I was very satisfied with the service at your restaurant."*

*"Quality tech support."*

*"I really enjoyed your product."*

Specific testimonials work for two reasons. First, they sound more credible. Second, they promote a specific benefit or address a question that may help persuade potential buyers.

## GOOD TESTIMONIALS OVERCOME SALES OBJECTIONS

That's right. Use testimonials that talk about objections. Some companies are afraid to use this kind of testimonial, yet they can be the most powerful tool in your arsenal. Testimonials from skeptics stand out because they sound credible. And by addressing and voicing what many prospective clients may be feeling, these testimonials are powerful persuaders.

Testimonials that address objections sound like this:

> *"When I first walked into your store, I thought I would be pressured into buying something, but I was very pleasantly surprised by how professional your sales team was. No pressure, no hard-sell. Thank you."*
>
> *"I've been in business for 7 years. I didn't think there was anything in your training course I didn't already know. But ultimately, I was surprised to learn valuable techniques I'd never considered before."*

A good testimonial is believable and credible. Aside from what the testimonial says, the people reading the testimonial must believe it is from a real person. One way to accomplish this to include as many of the following as possible: the client's name; profession; city; age (sometimes), company name & title (if B2B); and the number of years they have been a client. Too many people make the mistake of using a testimonial that looks like this:

> *"I loved your store and your service."– Jane S.*

**I would not use this type of testimonial... ever.**

## LEVELS OF TESTIMONIALS FROM BEST TO WORST

**#1 - The absolutely best testimonial is a VIDEO TESTIMONIAL,** which consists of a live human being - on camera - talking about how great your business is and how they benefit by being your client.

**#2- Picture of your customer with**

**FULL NAME**

**AGE, OCCUPATION, COMPANY NAME** (for B2B) - or any other descriptor that is important for your target audience.

**CITY, STATE**

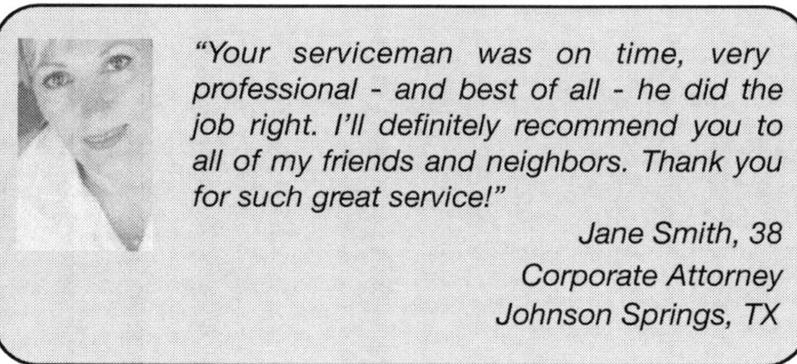


**#3- Same as above NO Photo**

**#4- Same as #3 but NO descriptor**

**FULL NAME**

**CITY, STATE**

Jane Smith

Johnson Springs, TX

As I said above, I would use nothing less than #4.

## OK... SO HOW DO YOU GET TESTIMONIALS?

What if you don't have any testimonials?

No problem; just ask for them. You'd be surprised how quickly you can create an assortment of great testimonials, especially if you have a good relationship with your clients and they're appreciative of what you do for them.

Go back to your past clients and ask them to give you a testimonial. Send them the Testimonial Form (below), run a testimonial contest. Ask your new clients coming in the door today to give you a testimonial immediately after you've completed the transaction. But you have to make it easy for them.

Today, with the iPhone there's no excuse for not getting video testimonials. I have a client that has carried a camera with him for years and taken videos of clients, pictures of them standing in front of their house (after he's installed new windows, siding or roofing) with his sign, a smile and a big thumbs up.

In fact, he takes this one step further, he uses those client testimonials in his sales presentations. When a prospect objects about price... he'll play a video of a customer who said the same thing before signing a contract. But, after they had the work done they say it was the best decision they made. He doesn't have to say anything... his customers are selling his jobs for him!

Give them a form (see example below) to answer standard questions that you prepare and make sure that it's okay to use them in your marketing materials. You must get their permission - IN WRITING - to use their name in any and all promotional material. Otherwise, you could be sued. That's why I include the permission statement right on

Testimonial Form

Name:____________________________________

Address:

City:________________ State:____________ Zip:________

Occupation:________________________________

Number of years as our client:________

What is your overall feeling about [business name]?________________

Describe in detail what part of your experience made you the happiest:

Describe the one or two most important benefits you've gotten the most from using [business name]... Please explain specifically what you've gained from the experience:

Thank you... We really appreciate your honest answers.

______I do not mind if you use my name and comments in any or all of your promotional materials.

Signature:________________________

Date:________________________

the form. If it's not signed, I get it signed. If they don't sign it, I don't use it. It's that simple.

On this book's website you'll find a couple of simple, easy-to-use client testimonial forms and a letter for you to download and adapt for your business to collect testimonials from your clients.

It's easy to get clients to fill this form out; here is one to give you an idea:

To wrap up, here are some ways of using testimonials in addition to placing them in your advertisements.

Pictures of your clients make your testimonials even more credible and effective. Also use pictures proving the comments made in the testimonials. For example, including a picture of a "before and after" use of your product or service (dirty carpet/clean carpet, old roof/new roof, before cosmetic procedure/after cosmetic procedure) is extremely powerful.

The ideal testimonial is a video. Up until this point, I have not talked at all about websites and the internet in this book, but this is the perfect place to use video of your clients raving about your product or service. If you were to collect a dozen of these video testimonials, you could burn them to a DVD and send it out with any marketing or sales materials you are currently using. You could use the videos on your website, or use them like my client does in his sales presentations.

You could take your testimonials and put them into a book. This works beautifully when the testimonials are in the client's own handwriting or in the form of a letter that they sent in to your business. The book could be a presentation book that you show to your prospects when you go to sell them. It could be a bound book that you mail to prospects. It could be a book that people can browse through while in your store.

I know of a speaker who doesn't write letters or have any marketing materials to send to prospects. What does he do? When someone calls his office and asks for information about a speaking engagement, he gets their name and address. He then sends them a (BIG) box full of what past clients have had to say about his previous speaking engagements.

That's all he does. No letter...nothing else.

He closes a huge number of prospects in a fiercely-competitive business based solely on the power of testimonials.

I know of a company that sells sheds in northern California. These aren't your typical Home Depot sheds; these are very cool structures like playhouses for kids, home offices and artists' studios. Their marketing materials are designed almost exclusively using testimonials from their clients. They use this strategy brilliantly. Each of the testimonials is actually a story about how his client is using their shed. They even went so far as to put the testimonials together into an infomercial-style video.

I created a one-sheet for one of my clients that is 3 columns of testimonials, with one big one (the best one) in the middle. There were 25 in all, with this heading at the top: "Here is what a few of our clients had to say about ..."

We used this in two ways. First, it was the back of a flyer that was distributed in the newspaper, and secondly, I had them blow up the flyer and put it in their window so the people passing by would get an opportunity to read what 25 people (just a few) had to say about their business.

For one of my clients we created a beautiful coffee table book called: "Distinctive Landscapes of Southern California" with pictures and commentary on over a dozen high-end landscape projects. This book actually served 2 purposes. First, it was used as a gift to the client after a large-scale project was completed. We would put the client's project on the cover and as the first "profiled" project in the book. Second, it's used as a sales tool. Of course with each profiled project was an actual and implied endorsement from the homeowner.

Think about how powerful it would be if you were to take what 25 of your best clients had to say about you, and put it into a format and location for any and all of your prospective clients to see 24 hours a day, 7 days a week. These 25 clients would be spreading the word about you and your company in a compelling and credible way. Do you think that would lead to more new clients, sales and profits? You bet it would! This leads me to my last point.

**YOU CAN NEVER HAVE TOO MANY TESTIMONIALS.**

I wouldn't be surprised if you have a bunch of testimonials lying around your office right now in the form of unsolicited thank-you notes from your clients. It's time to pull them out and put them to good use. Get them out and let your clients tell the world about how great your business is.

Make collecting testimonials a standard operating procedure in your business. Let your staff know how important it is for the business to collect testimonials from your clients. Collect as many as you can; the more you have, the more options you have for "controlled" word-of-mouth marketing. And the more options you have for attracting new clients, the more options you have for selling more of your products and services.

# CHAPTER 12

## Double Your Profits STRATEGY #8: Educate For Dominance

What you're about to discover is an incredible marketing tool so powerful and effective—and so bullet proof— that I call it my "Secret Weapon".

WARNING: I almost left this chapter out because unlike the other strategies in this book, this one will require some work - and potentially some expense - on your part. However, it is so powerful that when executed properly, it will instantly put you in a position to dominate your marketplace, and quickly and easily make your competition irrelevant!

I've included this strategy in a very abridged version because I believe so strongly in this strategy that leaving it out would have been a huge disservice to you. I have used this strategy in every business I have owned and I almost always recommend it to clients. I've simplified it as best I can here without destroying its integrity.

Although I will do my best to show you step-by-step how to execute this strategy, you may still require some additional assistance. At the end of the chapter you will find a number of resources to help you implement this powerful tool in your business.

This one strategy is so powerful that it can not only increase the effectiveness of your advertising by 5, 10 or more times, but it will give you an "unfair" advantage over all of your competitors. It could have such a dramatic impact on your business - in the form of additional phone calls, sales presentations, foot traffic, requests for service, etc. - that your infrastructure may not be able to handle the additional business it produces. Of all the strategies in this book, this is the only one that has the potential to completely transform your business and your life. Let's get started.

**Here's How To Instantly Position Yourself As The Authoritative Expert In Your Field So You'll Get More Motivated Prospects Calling You In A Month Than You Currently Get All Year !**

Let me ask you a question: *"Do you consider yourself an expert in your field?"* I am going to make the assumption and/or argument here that you are... and in more ways than you think.

With this strategy, we are going to take that expertise and put it to use. We are going to reposition you and your business as THE industry expert in your market.

How are we going to do this?

You are going to supply the information that helps eliminate your prospective clients' fears, builds their confidence and objectively educates them, making you STAND APART as the sole provider of your product or service who cares enough to give them what they really want and need...information, advice and confidence.

You will instantly go from being just another person who is trying to separate them from their money to their Trusted Advisor. Done properly, you become the preferred provider for all their needs from that day forward.

Would you agree then that becoming your clients' Trusted Advisor in your particular field could result in a dramatic increase in profits? You bet it could!

But Brian, "How can I be considered THE expert? Aren't trusted advisers usually doctors or lawyers? I'm just a ______________!"

If you're like most business owners, you believe that this strategy only works for "professionals" like CPA's, doctors or attorneys... but you're WRONG!

You may believe that their profession is more of a 'Trusted Advisor' profession than yours is. This couldn't be further from the truth. You see, the truth of it is that they provide a service or product just like you do. The fallacy is that because they have a piece of paper on their wall, they are somehow in a different category than you are or that their status is somehow greater than yours or mine... this is WRONG, WRONG, WRONG!

Over the years we've been conditioned to believe that those professionals - because of their fancy degrees - are somehow in a different category than the 'common man'. I may be offending those of you who are professionals, but that is not my intention. The advice that I am about to dispense applies just as much to you as it does to the shop owner, contractor, restaurant owner or any other business owner.

Aside from the "status" they theoretically possess, what's the difference between those professionals and us? The basic difference is that they are perceived as an expert... as being their clients' **Trusted Advisor**.

My brother-in-law is an attorney; I love him and respect him, but when it comes down to it, he's just like any other business owner. He has clients who expect certain things of him, he always has to be looking for new clients and new sales, he has to make payroll and he has overhead, etc., etc. The only difference is that his business model is different. While he may not be working under a car, installing a toilet or serving food, he's working just as hard as you are. And when I say just as "hard" I mean "manual-labor hard". Just because he deals with paper, telephone and computers, it still represents manual labor.

And he'll be the first to tell you that he is just like any other business person, except that his clients regard him as an expert; he is their Trusted Advisor.

What you must realize is that you too are a professional and your clients seek out your business not only to buy products/services from you, but for your advice, expertise, knowledge and guidance just like they do from the other 'professionals'. There is absolutely no reason why you can't be your clients' Trusted Advisor for whatever products or services your business offers.

If you want them to view you the same way, treat you the same way, take your advice in the same way, and pay you in the same way... you can do it, and it's a whole lot easier than you think!

The sad truth is that most business owners don't see it this way and therefore don't provide the required guidance. As a Trusted Advisor, your clients will give you more respect, more money and more business than you ever dreamed possible.

So now you may be thinking: "But those guys went to school; they have diplomas or certifications, I don't have any of that." I'll let you in on a little secret about achieving Trusted Advisor status: it's not something that you have to get certified for; it doesn't require a degree from a university or permission from any nominating body; and it does not require any time or money. This is one of the few things in life that is "magically bestowed" upon you and it can be done almost instantly.

**"How's that?" you ask.**

## EASY... YOU BESTOW IT UPON YOURSELF!

You storm the palace... throw out the old ineffective king... take his crown... put in on your head and declare to the world that you are the new king!

You've paid the price to learn your specialty; this strategy is about capitalizing on that expertise. The information that you've spent years learning and developing (and probably take for granted), is worth a fortune to your clients. Remember at the beginning of this chapter I made the assumption that you are an expert in your field? Well now you know why! Whether you want to believe it or not, you're already an expert in your field.

Now we just have to take that expertise and put it into a format that repositions you and your business. How do we do that?

## OFFER YOUR PROSPECTS WHAT THEY REALLY WANT & NEED:

## INFORMATION, ADVICE & CONFIDENCE

I believe that the cornerstone of a good marketing strategy should be to educate your clients and prospects. When you educate your clients, you'll see your profits soar because an educated client is more loyal, easier to sell to and willing to pay a fair (often times premium) price for your product or service.

So as the newly-crowned expert in your field and in your marketplace, you provide the information that teaches your clients the "insider secrets" of your industry... secrets that they couldn't learn any other way (or at least not very easily). You deliver the information to them in a concise, simple, easy-to-understand format and you hold nothing back. You make sure that you reveal every tip, strategy or dirty little secret of that industry and you educate them on how to get the best value or experience from your type of business.

The more "insider" information your clients know about your field or industry, the more money they'll spend, and the more they'll be willing to spend with you—their recognized expert. The value they place on this specialized information instantly catapults you to "expert" status.

Stop and think about this for a minute: How much specialized knowledge do you possess that would be of value to your clients or potentials clients? Regardless of what kind of business you own, I trust that at a minimum you know the right way to buy from that business.

For example, if you are a contractor of any kind, don't you know how contractors rip people off? Don't you know what makes a job good, how contractors take shortcuts and what makes a quality job? If you are a roofer, doesn't part of your sales pitch include why your company is better than the next guy's? Doesn't some of that presentation or pitch come from your "insider" knowledge of the roofing business?

What about a restaurant owner? I'm not a big wine drinker (frankly I don't really get the whole "wine" thing), but I understand that in some cases a good glass (or bottle!) of wine can really enhance a meal. My guess is that most people have never really been educated on this. What if a restaurant owner educated people on what type of wine complements a certain type of food?

What about an auto repair center of any kind? Do I even need to go over the possibilities of this one... or new or used car dealers?

How To Finance Your New (Or Used) Vehicle.

How To Negotiate For Your New (Or Used) Car.

Discover 6 Ways New (Or Used) Car Dealers Rip You Off, And How To Avoid Them!

What if you sold men's or ladies' wear, jewelry or other products based on personal tastes, body shapes, lifestyle, etc.? Couldn't you provide information on what makes a men's (or ladies') suit fit just right... the right type of shirt to wear with a particular suit... when a watch is too big for someone's wrist... or how to select the "right" diamond? I could go on for hours. Don't you think that the general public would find this information useful?

Let me say it again: Regardless of what business you are in... no matter how mundane or ordinary you may think your business is... whether you sell to businesses or consumers... you possess the knowledge and expertise to educate your clients (and future clients) and make them think of you as their first... their best... their ONLY choice. You become the sole provider they can <u>trust</u>, <u>respect</u>, and <u>turn to</u>.

Now you may be thinking that since all of this information is available on the internet, they won't want it from you when they can just turn on their computer. Not true. Remember... people don't want to do research; they just want to get to the truth as quickly as possible. They are looking for an expert... they are looking for someone to stand up and say "I know this subject better than anyone"... they're looking for YOU!

So what does this physically look like?

Typically the information you provide is contained in a value-packed, information-rich format like a printed book or booklet (eBook, or special report online) that gives your reader the information and then includes actionable steps they can take to achieve their desired outcome. The information can also be in the form of articles submitted to newspapers, magazines, newsletters or trade publications that your prospect reads, in recorded messages or in "live" seminars.

For our purposes here, we are going to focus on the printed book or booklet. We generally call these "consumer guides," or "free reports." I have used both books and booklets and called them "reports" and "consumer guides." Depending on the type of business you own and your expectations, one can work just as well as the other.

So, how do you feel about writing a book or booklet? I can already hear the moans and groans of dismissal: "I can't write a book." Or "I don't have time to write a book." Don't worry; it's not nearly as hard as you think! In just a few minutes I'm going to show you how to do it yourself, or - if you don't want to do it yourself - I'll show you how you can get this completely done for you, for a lot less money than you think! For now, let's continue.

In Strategy #5 we talked about direct-response advertisements. Specifically, we discussed adding powerful headlines to your ads to generate more attention and interest. With this strategy we are adding the next most important component to your ad, and that is an irresistible offer - a reason for your prospective client to get up off the couch and take action!

In this case, your offer to your prospective clients is for a FREE consumer guide or report. This guide or report will educate them on how they can gain, save, profit, achieve or accomplish something through your product or service. It will show how the product or service will increase mental, physical, financial, social, spiritual or intellectual well-being, satisfaction or fulfillment. But most importantly, it will show the reader how to avoid, reduce or eliminate problems, risks, difficulties, worries or fears by using your product.

**(Before moving forward, you may want to read that paragraph again.)**

And because the information in the consumer guide or report will be timely and of value to them, you will get them to raise their hand and let you know that they are interested in your product or service. Then they will be more likely to provide you with additional information about themselves (name, address, email address, etc.) than they would have if you were simply asking them to buy something, or - even worse - not offering anything at all. Part of the beauty of this strategy - and the reason I call it my "secret weapon" -- is because you will even attract the prospects who were thinking about buying from your competition!

For example, here is a book I created for a landscape company:

Here is a booklet we did for a private training gym client:

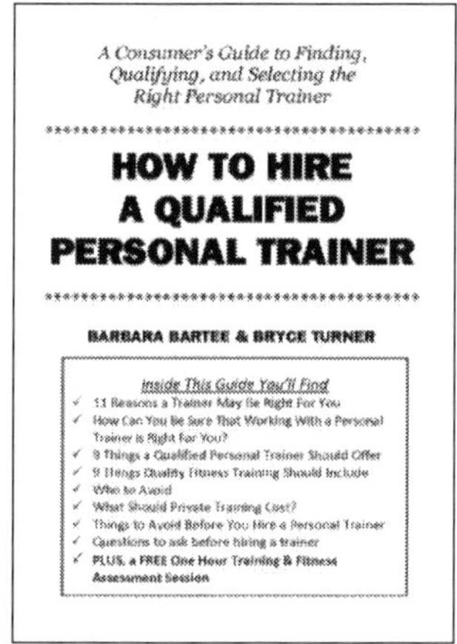


I've done hundreds of these for the home improvement industry. And done one for almost every client I've worked with. By the way, both of the above examples are available at this book's site for you to download, study and "steal" ideas from.

Ultimately I want to use this system to capture valuable information about every prospect with even a fleeting interest in buying your product or service in your market, because by capturing their information I can consistently <u>nurture them</u> along until they are ready to buy.

## WHY DOES THIS SYSTEM WORK SO EFFECTIVELY AS A PROFIT-INCREASING TOOL?

This system works because you position yourself as a source of help, valuable information, advice and education for their "problem", rather than someone blatantly trying to sell them something.

You're offering information in a "package" (a book), that is perceived to be authoritative and credible.

You are offering this information in a non-threatening environment. Rather than making someone call your office and speak with a live human being (and risk feeling foolish, stupid or pressured into an appointment), they simply need to leave a message on a prerecorded voicemail or sign up via your website.

The best part is that it works beautifully in every kind of business or industry!

## ACTION STEPS:
## A SIMPLE FORMULA FOR WRITING A CONSUMER GUIDE

Here are the 10 steps to put this strategy to work for you - by the way, we charge tens of thousands of dollars to create systems like this for clients. What I've laid out below gives you an ultimate shortcut. But just like most everything in this book if you don't execute it, you can't possibly benefit from it. Remember, the majority of people (including your competition) will look at this and think it's too much work, or that it won't "work" in their business, or they'll get to it another time. This gives you an enormous opportunity to stand out from the crowd and grow your business and your profits in ways that you've only dreamed of.

$$

**STEP 1:** Get yourself a small digital voice recorder and then put yourself in this scenario: you live on the west coast and your best friend lives on the east coast. Your best friend calls you and needs the same product or service you sell, but you can't provide it to him/her from the west coast. What advice, council or guidance would you give your friend so that when he walks into a place of business he is armed and ready to get the best service and the best deal?

And/or, record up to 5 of your company's sales presentations; it can include you - or your best salesperson - delivering the presentation, .

**STEP 2:** Once you have the recordings, get them transcribed. The transcription will come to you in a Word document.

**STEP 3:** Edit the document into a small guide that adheres to the format that follows.

Present the problem that your business solves for the prospective client. Remember that your presentation must explain how he can gain, save, profit, achieve or accomplish something through your product or service. Or, show how the product or service will increase mental, physical, financial, social, spiritual or intellectual well-being, satisfaction or fulfillment. Show the reader how to avoid, reduce or eliminate problems, risks, difficulties, worries or fears by using your product.

Present your solutions based on your expertise and "insider" information. IMPORTANT NOTE: The book or guide must be educational and informational for the consumer; it should give them advice and guidance on how to benefit from your type of business.

However, it is still a sales tool and it has a job; its job is to get you a new client! So it must sell you and/or your company. You have to be careful how you do this. The mistake that people often make with this strategy is to make it all about them, instead of about the potential client. After each section or tip, they'll add "XYZ Company does it this way" or they'll put their company logo on it. Trust me; you will lose credibility and the effectiveness of this strategy by doing that. Your report must look and sound as "official" and unbiased as possible.

Your book or guide does not need to be a blatant sales pitch for you. If written properly, all roads point to you and/or your company as the only obvious choice. At the end of the guide or book you will have an "About the Author" section, an "About the Company" section and a "FREE GIFT FROM THE AUTHOR" page. This is where the selling will happen.

Give the reader a step-by-step action plan for getting the best service and the best deal.

At the end of the guide, include information about the author (you) and your business.

The two books shown above are at this book's website (see "Resources" below) and are provided for you to use as a model or template.

NOTE: You can have these written for you by hiring someone from elance.com or guru.com.

**STEP 4:** Before you finalize the document, read it out loud. Make sure it makes sense. Edit any sections of the document that don't flow well.

**STEP 5:** Finalize the document and have a small quantity printed and ready.

**STEP 6:** Create an offer and include it in all of your advertisements, business cards, brochures and store windows. Advertise the book or guide and the benefits the client will gain by reading the guide. (You can refer back to Chapter 9 regarding headlines to come up with titles for your book)

**STEP 7:** Offer the guide for free to any prospective client. But make them fill out an information card so you'll capture all of their information.

IMPORTANT: NEVER, NEVER just hand it to someone who asks you for it. Have a card or form that they must fill out in order to get the information. Remember, you want the prospect's information so you can market to them. There is no point in just handing it to anyone who asks. (By the way, this is also a surefire way of cheapening the material and making it totally ineffective!)

**STEP 8:** Once you have captured their information, enter that information into your marketing database and mail them the book or report. Include a cover letter that thanks them for requesting the report. Remind them what is contained in the report and let them know that you are available if they need help or counsel. (I know this may cost a little more, but it will be worth the added expense.)

**STEP 9:** Follow up 10 days after you've sent the report with a simple letter making sure they received it and to remind them that you and your staff are available to answer any of their questions.

In the P.S. of your letter you'll want to add an offer for them to come into your store, office, practice, restaurant or call for service.

**STEP 10:** You need to follow up constantly with the prospects you attract. Their names are on your mailing list. At 3-, 4- or 5-month intervals send further information with another follow-up letter saying: "We thought you might be interested in this. Anytime you need our help or counsel or you want to visit, we will be pleased to help you." You'll also want to put these people into your other ongoing communications like your company newsletter.

# SECTION FOUR

## PUTTING IT TOGETHER FOR MAXIMUM PROFIT!

*"Success doesn't come from doing what everyone else does. Success comes from the willingness to do what others won't do."*

- Brian Kaskavalciyan

# CHAPTER 13

## TO DOUBLE YOUR PROFITS YOU MUST TAKE ACTION!

So here we are almost at the end, but really this is just the beginning and you have a choice to make: Do you take the advice from this book and apply it to your business, or do you put it aside for another day?

I am certain that if you take the advice you will see incredible results.

But if you keep doing exactly what you're doing now, you'll continue to get the same results you're getting now. So you need to decide what you are going to do - now - before you put this book down, never to return to it again.

The number one thing that I find holds all of us back is just getting started. Often times we don't get started because we don't know what to do or how to do it and unfortunately, nothing happens unless we start, unless we take ACTION!

So let me suggest a step-by-step action plan to help you get started implementing the tactics and strategies in this book. On the following pages is a tool called the Double Your Profit Success Workbook™ that can be found and downloaded for your use on this book's website.

I'll walk you through each of the steps and then introduce you to the workbook at the end of the chapter.

## STEP 1

First we need to decide which areas of your business we are going to start working on. To do this, we need to determine exactly where we are now. Since this book is about profit, we are going to focus solely on numbers that affect sales and profits.

On the following page is a table that I have started with the basic information found for most businesses. Your job is to write in the actual numbers from your business under the CURRENT column. I have intentionally left a number of blank spaces for you to fill in the important numbers in your business that affect sales and profits. For example, there is likely some sales-conversion rate that should be tracked in your business, price or markup, traffic counts, etc. You should list here all of the important numbers that effect your sales and profits.

Next, come up with a new set of numbers for 6 months from today (this can be any time period of 3 months, 12 months or 24 months). These are your target numbers - the new outcomes you want for your business.

At this point you should not change every number; just pick a couple to begin with. It will be tempting to just change the net profit number; however, that will not give us enough information to work with. Net profit is an effect of changes made to the other numbers. If you get stuck, go back to the worksheets you filled out earlier in the book to help you come up with the new numbers. Or, go to The Profit Blaster Matrix at www.DoubleYourProfitBook.com and use that tool to help.

| | CURRENT | 6 MONTHS |
|---|---|---|
| SALES | | |
| GROSS PROFIT MARGIN | | |
| LVC (FROM CHAPTER 3) | | |
| AVERAGE TRANSACTION VALUE | | |
| FREQUENCY OF PURCHASE | | |
| NUMBER OF CLIENTS | | |
| | | |
| | | |
| | | |
| | | |
| | | |
| NET PROFIT | | |

NOTE: This table appears as the SCORECARD in the Double Your Profit Success Workbook.

The numbers in the right column are your outcomes (goals). These are the numbers that we are going to work toward.

## STEP 2

Now that we know your new outcome numbers, next we need to decide which strategies and tactics we are going to use to get to the new outcomes. In this book I introduced you to 8 strategies and within those 8 strategies are at least 21 tactics for getting the job done. It's time now to select the strategy and tactic(s) we are going to focus on to achieve the outcome.

Here is a summary of the strategies and tactics introduced to you in this book:

#1 - Fencing in Your Herd

- Collect Prospect/Client Data
- Acknowledge & Appreciate
- Communicate

#2 - Increase the Frequency of Purchase

- Lock in the Next Appointment
- Monthly Newsletter
- Cash Flow Surge

#3 - Increase the Average Transaction Value

- The Bump
- The Up-sell

#4 - Raise Your Prices

- Single Product/Service
- Across the Board

#5 - Use Only Direct-Response Advertising

- Headline
- Benefits
- Offer

#6 - Use Big, Bold Guarantees

- The Time Guarantee
- The Negative-Trait Guarantee
- Risk-Reversal Guarantee

#7 - Use Testimonials

- Get Testimonials
- Insert Testimonials into Ads

#8 - Educate For Dominance

- Write Consumer Guide
- Free Recorded Message
- Write a Book

STRATEGY

______________________________

TACTIC

______________________________

Next, let's figure out what the outcome looks like when it is accomplished. Write out in detail what it will look like when it is done. To give you an idea of what this looks like, take a look at the example below:

STRATEGY

#2 INCREASE THE FREQUENCY OF PURCHASE

TACTIC

LOCK IN THE NEXT APPOINTMENT

WHAT DOES "DONE" LOOK LIKE? WHAT IS THE PROFIT IMPACT?

STAFF ASKING FOR NEXT APPOINTMENT AT COMPLETION OF EVERY TRANSACTION.

1 OUT OF 3 CLIENTS BOOKING NEXT APPOINTMENT, RESULTING IN A 16% INCREASE IN REVENUE AND AN ADDITIONAL $39,000 IN PROFIT.

## STEP 3

Now that we know the strategy, the tactic(s) and the outcome we want, next we need to put together a game plan. We'll do this by first listing the actions, tasks or steps you'll need to take to accomplish your outcome.

Next, what will it take in terms of time, money and resources? Here are some questions that might help you accomplish the tasks:

- How long will it take you in hours to accomplish this task?

- How much money will it take to accomplish the task?

- Who can help accomplish the task?

- By what date will this task be complete?

Once you've got the action steps listed, I like to gauge your commitment to getting them done. Next to each task put a little "Y" for yes or "N" for no. If you look at the task and cannot commit to it, then you must determine how critical the completion of that task is to the overall result. If it is critical, can you find someone else to do it for you? Can you modify it in a way that gets you more excited and ultimately committed? Remember back in Chapter 1 I suggested that unless you are fully committed to the outcome there is no way it will be accomplished. You will give up long before you've achieved the outcome.

We only get what we commit to.

# STEP 4

Finally, it's time to take ACTION! Go through the list you've created and prioritize the action steps. You can start with (1) or start with (A); it doesn't matter. Once you've got your list, get to work. Work until you've got the task completed and then move on to the next one.

At this stage you also want to carefully monitor your progress. Once you implement the strategy or tactic, you will undoubtedly test different actions. Watch for what's working and what's not. Quickly change what isn't working until you get the result you want.

**PROFIT RESOURCE**

Go to www.DoubleYourProfitBook.com and download the **Double Your Profit Success Workbook.**

I've put together a success workbook for you. On the following pages are what this workbook looks like. It is designed for you to use on a weekly or monthly basis to help keep you on track, working towards your intended outcomes, using the concepts, tools, strategies and tactics from this book. I suggest printing out a few copies and begin using this powerful tool right away.

## PAGE 1

# *Double Your Profit Success Workbook*™

*"For every disciplined effort*
*there are multiple rewards."*

NAME ______________________ DATE ______________________

### My Company Outcomes — Date

FILL IN THE OUTCOMES YOU WANT FOR YOUR BUSINESS THIS MONTH/QUARTER/YEAR

1. ______________________ ________
2. ______________________ ________
3. ______________________ ________

MAKE IT HAPPEN

### This Week, I Will Focus On The Following Results:

FILL IN THIS WEEKS ACTION ITEMS FROM PAGE 3 INSIDE

1. ______________________
   ______________________
2. ______________________
   ______________________
3. ______________________
   ______________________

**Which action, if implemented this week, would have the biggest positive impact on your business and/or life?**

# PAGE 2

| STEP 1: THE OUTCOME<br>*WHAT IS YOUR INTENDED OUTCOME?* | *6 MONTHS FROM NOW HOW WILL YOUR LIFE BE DIFFERENT/BETTER AS A RESULT OF THIS OUTCOME?* |
|---|---|
| | BE DO HAVE |

| STEP 2: SELECT STRATEGY/TACTIC<br>*STRATEGY*<br>*TACTICS* | WHAT EFFECT WILL THIS HAVE ON YOUR BUSINESS AND/OR YOUR LIFE?<br>*PROFIT IMPACT* | *WHAT WILL "DONE" LOOK LIKE?* |
|---|---|---|
| **#1 - Fencing in Your Herd**<br>- Collect Prospect/Client Data - Acknowledge & Appreciate - Communicate<br>- | $______ | |
| **#2 - Increase the Frequency of Purchase**<br>- Lock in the Next Appointment - Monthly Newsletter<br>- Cash Flow Surge<br>- | $______ | |
| **#3 - Increase the Average Transaction Value**<br>- The Bump - The Up-sell<br>- | $______ | |
| **#4 - Raise Your Prices**<br>- Single Product/Service - Across the Board<br>- | $______ | |
| **#5 - Use Only Direct Response Advertising**<br>- Headline - Benefits - Offer<br>- | $______ | |
| **#6 - Use Big, Bold Guarantees**<br>- The Time Guarantee - The Negative Trait Guarantee<br>- Risk Reversal Guarantee<br>- | $______ | |
| **#7 - Use Testimonials**<br>- Get Testimonials - Insert Testimonials Into Ads<br>- | $______ | |
| **#8 - Educate For Dominance**<br>- Write Consumer Guide - Free Recorded Message<br>- Write Book<br>- | $______ | |

## PAGE 3

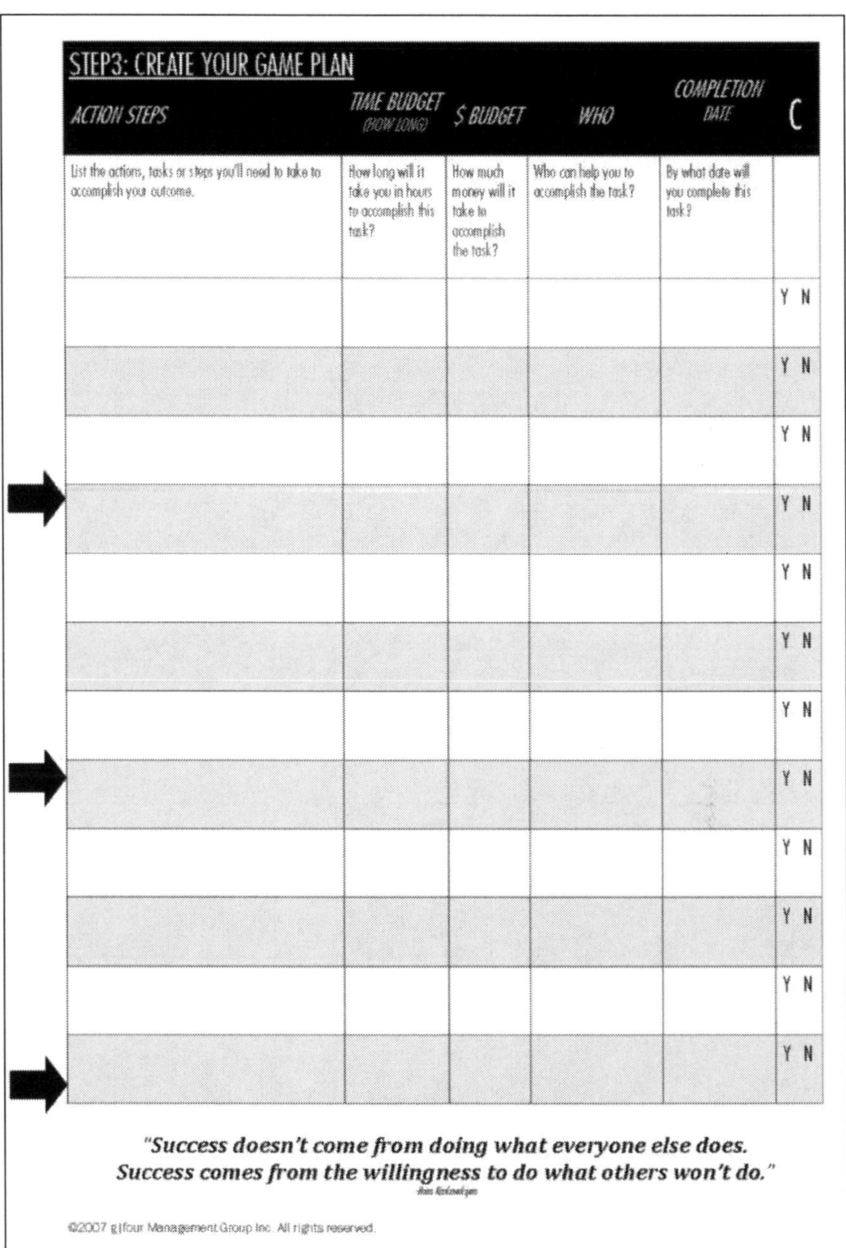

**STEP3: CREATE YOUR GAME PLAN**

| ACTION STEPS | TIME BUDGET (HOW LONG) | $ BUDGET | WHO | COMPLETION DATE | C |
|---|---|---|---|---|---|
| List the actions, tasks or steps you'll need to take to accomplish your outcome. | How long will it take you in hours to accomplish this task? | How much money will it take to accomplish the task? | Who can help you to accomplish the task? | By what date will you complete this task? | |
| | | | | | Y N |
| | | | | | Y N |
| | | | | | Y N |
| | | | | | Y N |
| | | | | | Y N |
| | | | | | Y N |
| | | | | | Y N |
| | | | | | Y N |
| | | | | | Y N |
| | | | | | Y N |
| | | | | | Y N |
| | | | | | Y N |

*"Success doesn't come from doing what everyone else does. Success comes from the willingness to do what others won't do."*

## PAGE 4

The primary PURPOSE of my business is to serve my life. My business is a TOOL for expanding my personal FREEDOM. Profit is the FUEL that allows me to achieve my DREAMS.

### STEP 4: SCORECARD

Enter the areas that effect sales and profits What is the CURRENT number(s)? The result you want in X months and TODAYS variance.

| | CURRENT | ____ MONTHS | VARIANCE |
|---|---|---|---|
| GROSS SALES | | | |
| GROSS PROFIT MARGIN | | | |
| LVC | | | |
| AVERAGE TRANSACTION VALUE | | | |
| FREQUENCY OF PURCHASE | | | |
| NUMBER OF CLIENTS | | | |
| | | | |
| | | | |
| | | | |
| | | | |
| | | | |
| | | | |
| | | | |
| | | | |

*"There's always a way if you're committed."*

# CHAPTER 14

## SO NOW WHAT?

In this book I have given you 8 easy-to-implement marketing strategies, any one of which could double or triple your profits in the next 6 months. These strategies are based on the basic building blocks that I would use if I was to come into your business as your marketing consultant to quickly create additional profits for your business.

I hope I've challenged you to think differently about your business. I know that some of what I've laid out may seem radical to you or defy conventional wisdom; the truth of it is that I haven't even started with the advanced stuff.

> *"Always bear in mind that your own resolution to succeed is more important than any one thing."*
>
> **Abraham Lincoln**

The fact that you've read this book suggests you're not satisfied with the amount of profit you're currently earning and you want to do something about it.

I trust I've shown you enough to dramatically improve your sales, your profits, your business and your life. However, I want to remind you that the critical element of success is ACTION. Knowing is not enough; you must now DO. And in order to do you must be clear on your outcome and why you want it... you must have a game plan... you must believe in the outcome... be motivated and fully committed... and then take ACTION on your game plan!

In just a minute, I'm going to give you a final "tip" that I believe can dramatically transform your business and your life, as it has for me and many others I know. But first, I thought it would be wise to spend a few minutes discussing why people fail.

## THE 5 BIGGEST REASONS PEOPLE FAIL

### 1. They Don't Do Anything

This is the number one reason why people fail - they don't do anything!

This is a killer. How can anyone possibly succeed if they don't do anything?

They can't.

So why do so many people do nothing?

I think a big reason is because they are afraid. Fear of failure, fear of success, fear of the unknown - it's all the same and you need to work through it.

It's normal to be afraid to try something different. Every successful person has taken action despite their fears.

I have failed many, many times. It sucks! I hate it, but you know what? I learn from my failures and I move on. In fact, I'll go so far as to say that had I never failed, I could never have succeeded! You'll almost always learn more from your failures than you will from your successes.

Don't be a victim of 'not doing anything'.

Do something! Take action despite your fear.

If you need help, there are plenty of resources in this book, on this book's website and on my website to help you out!

### 2. They Do Everything Half-Way

This is another big reason people fail. They get excited about all the different marketing strategies and start a whole bunch of them at once. They never give enough time to each one. They do all of them half-way. Then they wonder why nothing works!

If you have your hand in too many things, none of them will be profitable.

Pick 1 or 2 strategies to start with. Concentrate on one marketing strategy at a time. Get that one working and then start another. Once you have those going, pick the next one or two.

Don't try to do too much at once.

### 3. They Aren't Consistent

One of the reasons these marketing strategies work so well is that you apply them consistently. They are systems. You need to do every part of the system to get it to run correctly.

People are shocked when they just do the first step and it doesn't work as well as they wanted.

Would you be surprised if you put a DVD in your player and nothing happened? Of course not. You know you have to plug it in, hook it up to the TV, put the TV on the correct channel and then press play. Then (usually) it plays. Not before.

Well, it's the same way with any system, including a marketing system. There are several parts to make the systems work.

They work; you just have to work them.

### 4. They Have No Plan

Success never happens by accident. Not once. You have to have a plan. If you don't have a plan, you are subject to circumstances and life just happening to you, rather than you proactively creating what happens to you.

You must plan success. Plan how much you want to make and what strategies you are going to use to make that much. Planning isn't a big secret; it just takes time and commitment.

I've heard people say they didn't want to plan because they might change their minds. This is absurd. You can always alter your plan. Make your goals (outcomes) higher or lower. Pick a completely different outcome, but if you don't have a plan you'll never get anywhere.

If you keep doing what you've always done, you'll keep getting the results that you've always gotten. PLAN! PLAN! PLAN!

### 5. Procrastinate

Procrastination is a common reason people fail.

'I'll get around to it tomorrow' has destroyed more businesses than you can imagine.

And don't make excuses like:

"This won't work in my business."

"I don't know which neighborhoods are good so I'll just wait."

"I don't know exactly how to do this."

"I don't have ______ in place, I'll start when I have that."

So what if everything isn't perfect. It's much more important to do something than to wait for everything to be perfect. It won't happen.

Do your best. Give it a shot.

Then learn and improve.

Procrastination is deadly.

Don't wait.

Do it today!

If you can overcome all of these obstacles and set well-defined outcomes, it will enable you to direct your efforts and focus your energy toward something that's important to you. The system laid out in this book gives you a target to aim for and enables you to develop the self-discipline to continue working toward your target rather than becoming distracted and going off in other directions.

## ARE YOU READY TO DOUBLE YOUR PROFITS IN SIX MONTHS OR LESS?

We've come a long way with this book; to quickly recap:

In the first section - **Setting the Stage for Dramatically Increasing Your Profits** - we started off by discussing how we really get what we want, then talked about the "real" business you are in, the real value of a customer and the 3 ways to grow a business.

In the second section - **Uncovering the Hidden Riches Lying Dormant and Neglected Within Your Business** - I introduced you to the first 4 strategies for doubling your profits: fencing in your herd; increasing the frequency of clients' purchases; increasing your average transaction size and raising your prices.

In the third section - **How to Effectively and Profitably Acquire New Clients** - I introduced you to 4 strategies to help you attract more new clients; these strategies were: use only direct response advertising; use big, bold guarantees; use testimonials and the use of education to dominate your market.

In this last section - **Putting It All Together for Maximum Profit** - I introduced you to a tool called the Double Your Profit Success Workbook to help you put it all together to take action and go double your profits in six months or less.

So quite frankly, at this point you don't have any excuses for NOT doubling your profits; you have the tools and resources to do just that. However, the one thing that you need is to embrace the idea of working "on" your business, rather than "in" your business. Now this is a big part of my coaching with clients and the topic of a whole other book. In fact, if you want to read the best one on the subject read "The E-Myth" by Michael Gerber.

For our purposes here I'm just going to give you a quick introduction. If you want more help and resources for this you can contact the g|Four office. (Contact information is in the back of the book.)

## WORK "ON" YOUR BUSINESS, NOT "IN" YOUR BUSINESS

What the heck does this mean?

Working "in" your business refers to answering the phone, fulfilling orders - packing boxes, pricing jobs, running print jobs (if you own a print shop), cooking food, cleaning carpet, installing faucets (if you own a plumbing company), paying bills and managing employees. Any of these things are working "in" your business.

Working "on" your business is about strategy, planning, creating systems and implementation. Planning what service you want to add, creating your advertising, developing a marketing plan and executing it, developing an improved sales system, deciding on what items to stock, how to fill your restaurant, how to optimize your pricing, etc.

Get the difference?

Many of you probably spend most of your time working in your business now. That's okay, but you also need to work on your business. If you don't, no one else will. You need to plan to be successful. You need to plan in order to accommodate growth.

As your business grows and gets bigger, you should work less and less in your business. You should hire others to do the "work." You can't hire anyone to work on your business. You have to do that in order to be successful.

This is a powerful strategy.

The best way to differentiate between working "in" versus "on" is that you can generally hire someone to do the "in" functions and - depending on the type of business - this could be as low as $8 an hour. This is the strategy behind many of the most successful businesses anywhere in the world and the same strategy will work for you too. In fact, this is what I have discovered to be the biggest weakness of business owners and often they will readily admit it.

So here is what you do. Take just 2 hours every week at a pre-set day and time and have all your calls held. Lock your office door and work on your business.

- ✓ Work ON your marketing and advertising.
- ✓ Work ON your sales programs.
- ✓ Work ON improving the way you recruit, hire, train and develop your team.

Work ON anything that can substantially improve your business and increase your profits.

If you don't have a quiet place in your business, stay home, go to the library, go to a friend's office or go rent another office. Basically, just go anywhere that you won't be interrupted or disturbed.

You will fight this at first. It will not be easy to quiet the voices screaming at you to get back to work (trust me I've been there!), but you must work through it. Eventually the voices will quiet down and allow you to think, create and plan.

Believe me when I tell you - this will be the most profitable use of your time! If you do this simple task, you will quickly reap HUGE dividends. In fact, the more you do it, the more you will find that your 2 hours a week will grow to 4 hours a week, and then to 1 day a week. Work less and less "in" and more and more "on" your business. **You'll soon discover that the less "work" you do, the more money you'll make**. Yes, you read that right. Ultimately of course, the goal is for the business to run completely independent of you.

**I couldn't wrap up this updated edition (especially in these economic times), without addressing a very important subject.**

And that is personal responsibility.

It amazes me how many people blame something outside themselves for their lot in life. Sure, some people have legitimate reasons, but they are a very small minority. The majority of people have only one thing standing in their way, and it's not the current president, Congress, their competition, gas prices or any other excuse they can come up with. The biggest reason why people fail is that they don't take responsibility for their part in getting what they truly want. And this includes many, many business owners.

As entrepreneurs, we have chosen a path that requires us to be responsible for generating revenue and profits for our business every day. This is no easy task. I have been doing this now (without interruption) all of my adult life... nearly 20 years. I am keenly aware of this responsibility. I know that if I have a good month it's my responsibility, and if I have a bad month, it's also my responsibility (or fault). If I don't live in the house I want, drive the car I want or go to the places I want to go, it's all MY responsibility. Success or failure at anything is MY responsibility.

There is great confidence, faith and hope in personal responsibility, as well as a measure of pride. Personal responsibility is a difficult concept for many to grasp. In these troubling times, more and more people are resigning their personal responsibility when they should be embracing it. It's unfortunate for them, but for those of us who take on this responsibility, there will always be an abundance of opportunity.

At the beginning of the book, I told you a few things I believe about you; let me repeat them again here:

- **You have everything you need right now to get everything you want.**
- **There is nothing inherently "wrong" with you that would prevent you from getting anything you truly want.**
- **Deep down inside, you know what you really, truly want.**
- **You absolutely deserve to be, do or have whatever you desire.**

This book is just one step on your journey. (I don't think you're here right now by accident). We have discussed enough here to not just increase your sales, but radically transform your business and your life. **What you do next is up to you**. If you are truly serious about making significantly more profit in your business (so you can fund your ideal lifestyle), you will study this book (and others like it) and take total responsibility for your outcome(s).

Remember that almost without exception, inside of every business are hidden riches... gold, platinum and diamond mines of opportunity that are just waiting to be intelligently and strategically cultivated to reap the rewards... yours included!

Anyone that knows me personally knows that I love the character of Rocky Balboa. The guy that comes from nowhere to become a champion. As we watch Rocky (and his alter ego Sylvester Stallone) age and mature there is a lot to learn. I'll leave you with part of a speech Rocky gives his son in the final movie:

> "Then the time comes for you to be your own man and take on the world, and you did. But somewhere along the line, you changed. You stopped being you. You let people stick a finger in your face and tell you you're no good. And when things got hard, you started looking for something to blame, like a big shadow.
>
> Let me tell you something you already know. The world ain't all sunshine and rainbows. It's a very mean and nasty place and I don't care how tough you are, it will beat you to your knees and keep you there permanently if you let it. You, me, or nobody is gonna hit as

hard as life. But it ain't about how hard ya hit. It's about how hard you can get hit and keep moving forward. How much you can take and keep moving forward. That's how winning is done!

Now if you know what you're worth then go out and get what you're worth. But ya gotta be willing to take the hits, and not pointing fingers saying you ain't where you wanna be because of him, or her, or anybody! Cowards do that and that ain't you! You're better than that! I'm always gonna love you no matter what. No matter what happens. You're my son and you're my blood. You're the best thing in my life. But until you start believing in yourself, you ain't gonna have a life."

**Sylvester Stallone as Rocky Balboa**

Scan this code with your Smartphone to watch the video on YouTube

So what does this all add up to?

That depends on you.

It's not enough to think; you must now become.

It's not enough to want; you must now do.

Aside from making you more money, I hope that this book has also opened your eyes and your mind to a whole new set of possibilities for your business and your life. And as I've told you throughout this book, this is just an introduction... just "the tip of the iceberg" as they say. I hope you will continue to learn about marketing and the powerful effect it can have on your business and on your life.

Now, go take ACTION! Be bold, have fun, make money and live your dreams. Be sure to let me know how you do; I will enjoy hearing your success stories!

# ABOUT THE AUTHOR

Brian is no stranger to hard work; by 15 years old he had already worked in a restaurant, as a paperboy and as a caddy at the prestigious Olympic Club in San Francisco, California.

At 15, he witnessed firsthand how downsizing, mergers, and layoffs in corporate America affected people and their families when the company his father worked for (for almost 20 years), was sold. He was lucky; he was offered a position with the new company, but it meant having to move his family from northern California to southern California.

But it didn't last; within 2 years the company shut the office down and his 54-year old father was out of work. It was this experience that planted the seeds of entrepreneurship in Brian.

He worked his way through high school then college by first working in a restaurant (starting as a dishwasher) and then working for a construction company as a commissioned sales person/designer.

After college, he went looking for his first business and found it in a carpet-dyeing franchise. He didn't have very much money but was able to make a deal with the franchisor and use a credit card to finance the business. The first year, Brian did everything from cleaning and dyeing carpet to accounting and sales. He quickly learned that the only way to make any real money was to focus on building the business and he did just that. His first step was to stop cleaning carpet and focus on sales and marketing. As a result, over the next 2 years his franchise became the largest on the west coast.

While in the carpet business, the franchisor created a bathtub-refinishing concept. Brian was intrigued and purchased the rights for his market. In less than 3 years - without ever refinishing a bathtub himself - not only was he the largest in the chain (of over 150), but he was one of the highest-priced and most-profitable providers in the country. As a result, the business was sold for a significant profit.

In 1999, he was approached by a local handyman about partnering up in a handyman business. In early 2000 Brian and his partner began a local handyman business, and in less than one year that little local business was generating over $1,000,000 in revenue.

With the success of the concept and Brian's marketing and franchising experience, he decided the time was right to franchise his own brand. In 2002 he developed the infrastructure and systems to turn that local business into a national franchise company. Over the next few years he built the company to over 30 franchisee-owned offices around the U.S. and Canada... plus 3 of their own offices. Being the ever-restless entrepreneur, Brian sold the company in early 2007 to focus on his real love of marketing.

Today, Brian is involved in a number of businesses, but his real passion is helping business owners of all kinds improve their profits and company value by focusing on effective marketing and profit development strategies. From start-ups to $50 million dollar enterprises, Brian has worked with and advised business owners in nearly two dozen different industries including mortgage, chiropractic, auto repair, restaurant, home improvement, health care, internet, consulting, coaching, retail and fitness training. He has also worked with professional practices such as accountants, lawyers and doctors.

His company - g|Four Marketing Group Inc. - provides strategic marketing products and services designed to build his clients' profitability and business value, while increasing their free time and quality of life.

Brian lives in Miami, Florida and is happily married (to Adi), and has 2 children (Sophie and Lena).

*You can reach Brian at:*
**g|Four Marketing Group Inc.**
**2828 Coral Way, Suite 308 | Miami, FL 33145 | (305) 856-8788**

Scan this code with your Smartphone to access the g|Four website

# SUMMARY OF PROFIT RESOURCES

# FREE READER RESOURCES

The following resources can all be found at:

**www.DoubleYourProfitBook.com/register**

- ✓ Making the Shift™ Worksheet
- ✓ LVC (Lifetime Value of a Client) Calculator ($17.00 value)
- ✓ The Profit Blaster Matrix™ ($37.00 value)
- ✓ Thank You Note and Letter Templates ($47.00 value)
- ✓ The Next Appointment Brainstorm™ Worksheet
- ✓ Cash Flow Surge Letter Templates (Retail, Professional, Restaurant and Service) ($69 each - $276.00 value)
- ✓ The Bump/Up-Sell Brainstorm™
- ✓ The Bump and Up-Sell Strategy Worksheet
- ✓ The Price Optimizer Matrix™ ($55.00 value)
- ✓ 12 Fill-In-The-Blank Headline Templates Workbook ($69.00 value)
- ✓ The Big, Bold Guarantee Worksheet™
- ✓ Testimonial Request Form (2) and Letter for Requesting Testimonials ($37.00 value)
- ✓ Full Book - "8 Insider Secrets Every Homeowner Considering Investing $100,000 Or More On A Landscape Project Must Know!" ($19.00 value)
- ✓ Full Consumer Guide - "How to Hire a Qualified Personal Trainer." ($19.00 value)

Scan this code with your Smartphone to register your book and unlock all of the resources.

Made in the USA
Middletown, DE
10 February 2017